Recipes from WASHINGTON

Cookbook Resources LLC
Highland Village, Texas

MW00667411

Recipes from Washington

Printed January 2011

International Standard Book Number: 978-1-59769-010-2

Library of Congress Number: 2010048142

Library of Congress Cataloging-in-Publication Data

    Recipes from Washington.
      p. cm.
    Includes bibliographical references and index.
    ISBN 978-1-59769-010-2
    1. Cooking, American--Pacific Northwest style. 2. Cooking--Washington (State) 3. Cookbooks. I. Cookbook Resources, LLC.
    TX715.2.P32R43 2010
    641.59797--dc22
                  2010048142

Cover by Nancy Murphy Griffith

Edited, Designed and Published in the United States of America
and Manufactured in China by
Cookbook Resources, LLC
541 Doubletree Drive
Highland Village, Texas 75077

Toll free 866-229-2665

www.cookbookresources.com

Bringing Family and Friends to the Table

The Agricultural Bounty of Washington

People living in Washington State today eat many of the same things the native Indians ate thousands of years ago. Plates are filled with more than 100 varieties of fresh salmon, trout, haddock, cod, king crab, clams, mussels, Dungeness crab, shrimp, oysters and geoducks.

Climates and soil combine to bring some of the best berries, apples, pears, potatoes, mushrooms, hops, sweet cherries, grapes, lentils, asparagus, apricots, sweet corn, carrots, wheat, barley, prunes, plums and dairy products anywhere in North America. Many varieties are the same that colonists brought from Europe and many are from the same varieties that grew wild along the rivers, coastline and valleys in this spectacular region.

From its vast wealth of home-grown fruits, vegetables, seafood and meats, the people of the Pacific Northwest have developed an appreciation for the quality of fresh flavors and the simplicity of great dishes. They consider natural flavors the best flavors and tend to turn away from heavy sauces and complicated herbs and spice mixtures.

What's better than fresh seafood steamed, broiled, grilled or pan-fried without a lot of fanfare and fancy touches? And what's better with ice cream than a simple red raspberry sauce or fresh apple pie?

The compilation of these recipes has been a joy to prepare because we concentrated on the bounty of this great state. We hope you enjoy them as much as we have.

—*The Editors*

Dedication

With a mission of helping you bring family and friends to the table, Cookbook Resources strives to make family meals and entertaining friends simple, easy and delicious.

We recognize the importance of sharing meals as a means of building family bonds with memories and traditions that will be treasured for a lifetime. Mealtime is an opportunity to sit down with each other and share more than food.

This cookbook is dedicated with gratitude and respect for all those who show their love with homecooked meals, bringing family and friends to the table.

Map of Washington

Contents

A Brief History of the Pacific Northwest and Washington State

The Pacific Northwest covered the northwest corner of North America and was inhabited by native Indian tribes as long as 13,000 years ago. The tribes' large populations gathered at the mouths of estuaries and along the Columbia River.

The area was rich with berries, nuts, wild vegetables, wild game and seafood of all kinds and provided its inhabitants with varied and sophisticated diets. Villages were large and houses were built with planks. Ornate totem poles were carved to record the history and traditions.

The first European to meet natives in the territory was Juan de Fuca, a Greek captain sailing under the Spanish flag, who visited the straits in 1773; the straits now bear his name.

In 1775 Bruno Heceta of Spain was the first to explore the territory. He was followed by Captain Robert Gray of America in 1792 and Captain George Vancouver of Great Britain with his officers Peter Puget and Joseph Whidbey who began charting Puget Sound that same year. The Spanish and Brits worked together to chart the coastline all the way from Oregon to the Alaskan Peninsula.

After Meriwether Lewis and William Clark reached the confluence of the Columbia and Snake Rivers in 1805, they opened the Oregon Trail to Europeans and Americans. Native American Indians stayed on their homelands and did not migrate to other areas. Conflicts and wars between the tribes and new settlers not devastating to the Indians, but they were almost wiped out from smallpox, measles and other diseases brought by the Europeans.

Spain ceded its original Pacific Northwest claims to the U.S. in the Transcontinental Treaty of 1819. The Oregon Territory included what is now Washington, Oregon and parts of Idaho and Montana.

In 1846 the British ceded its claims for what was called the Oregon Territory to the U.S. in the Treaty of Oregon. The northern border with Canada was established along the 49th parallel except for Vancouver Island. The Oregon Territory was divided into two areas; what is now called Washington had its southern border drawn along the Columbia River and the 46th parallel, dividing it from Oregon. Oregon became a state in 1859 and Washington became a state in 1889. Washington is the only state to be named after a U.S. President.

Originally the territory was called Columbia after the Columbia River, but it was changed to Washington after the first U.S. president to avoid confusion with the District of Columbia.

Today Washington's terrain, its people, industry and agriculture are some of the most varied in the U.S. The forests on the Olympic Peninsula are among the rainiest places in the world. Cape Flattery on Olympic Peninsula is the northwestern-most point in the 48 contiguous United States.

The San Juan Islands archipelago has 172 named islands and many unnamed islands in the Salish Sea just north of Puget Sound. The largest ferry system in the U.S. connects these islands to the mainland and carries more than 25 million people a year. It is ranked as the third largest in the world. The world's largest floating bridge connects Seattle with the cities on the east side of Lake Washington.

Olympia is the capital of Washington and is considered one of the most beautiful state capital settings in the U.S. Olympia sits on Budd Inlet which connects to Puget Sound, with picturesque views of Mount Rainier and the Olympic Mountain Range.

The Columbia River Gorge Scenic Byway is a stretch along the Washington-Oregon border that crosses thick forests and spectacular viewing areas of waterfalls and the Columbia River.

In the southwestern part of the state, Mount Rainier is the highest point in the state and contains excellent examples of old growth forest and subalpine meadows. Mount St. Helens is one of the world's most famous volcanoes since its eruption in 1980.

In the southeastern part of the state, Walla Walla, meaning many waters, is not far from the great Columbia River and the Blue Mountains. Vineyards, wheat fields and horse ranches dot the area today.

In the northeastern part of the state where the Columbia River carves out deep gorges, the Grand Coulee Dam stands as the largest dam and concrete structure in the U.S.

Washington's economy is dominated by aviation, software and technology, agricultural products, forest products, and commercial fishing. Washington produces more apples, raspberries, hops, pears, sweet cherries and spearmint oil than any other state in the U.S. It is one of the leading producers of lumber and wood products. It is second only to California in wine production in the U.S.

Washington National Parks and Sites

Name	Location
Ebey's Landing National Historical Reserve	Coupeville, Washington
Fort Vancouver National Historic Site	Vancouver, Washington
Klondike Gold Rush – Seattle Unit National Historical Park	Seattle, Washington
Lake Chelan National Recreation Area	Stehekin, Washington
Lake Roosevelt National Recreation Area	Canadian border going to Coulee Dam along the Columbia River, Washington
Lewis & Clark National Historic Trail	Idaho, Illinois, Iowa, Kansas, Missouri, Montana, Nebraska, North Dakota, Oregon, South Dakota, Washington
Mount St. Helens National Volcanic Monument	Amboy, Castle Rock, Washington
Mount Rainier National Park	Ashford, Enumclaw, Packwood, Wilkeson, Washington
Nez Perce National Historical Park	Idaho, Montana, Oregon, Washington
North Cascades National Park	Marblemount, Washington
Olympic Coast National Marine Sanctuary	Port Angeles, Washington
Olympic National Park	Port Angeles, Washington
Ross Lake National Recreation Area	Newhalem, Washington
San Juan Island National Historical Park	Friday Harbor, Washington
Whitman Mission National Historic Site	Walla Walla, Washington

Interesting facts and other information about Washington are marked with apples, the leading fruit crop of the state.

Snacks and Teasers

Washington Facts

State Vegetable: *Walla Walla Sweet Onion*

State Fruit: *Apple*

State Nickname: *The Evergreen State*

State Amphibian: *Pacific Chorus Frog*

Curry Lover's Veggie Dip

1 cup mayonnaise
½ cup sour cream
1 teaspoon curry powder
¼ teaspoon hot sauce
1 teaspoon lemon juice
Paprika
Raw vegetables

- Combine all ingredients (except paprika and vegetables) in bowl and mix until they blend well.

- Sprinkle a little paprika for color. Cover and refrigerate. Serve with raw vegetables. Yields 1½ cups.

Ginger Fruit Dip

1 (3 ounce) package cream cheese, softened
1 (7 ounce) jar marshmallow creme
½ cup mayonnaise
1 teaspoon ground ginger
1 teaspoon grated orange peel
Fresh fruit sticks

- Beat cream cheese in bowl on medium speed until smooth. Add marshmallow creme, mayonnaise, ginger and orange peel and stir until smooth.

- Serve with fresh fruit sticks. Yields 1½ cups.

The state of Washington is the only state to be named for an American president.

Ocean Park Roasted Garlic Dip

*Ocean Park is the home of the Northwest Garlic Festival held in June.
Garlic is not grown in the area, but people there celebrate all things garlic.*

4 - 5 whole garlic cloves
Olive oil
2 (8 ounce) packages cream cheese, softened
¾ cup mayonnaise
**1 (7 - 9 ounce) jar sweet roasted red peppers, drained, coarsely
    chopped**
1 bunch fresh green onions with tops, chopped
Red pepper or paprika
Chips

- Preheat oven to 400°.

- Lightly brush outside of garlic cloves with a little oil and place
  in shallow baking pan. Heat for about 10 minutes and cool.
  Press roasted garlic out of cloves and chop.

- Beat cream cheese and mayonnaise in bowl until creamy. Add
  roasted garlic, roasted peppers and green onions and mix well.
  (Roasted peppers are great in this recipe, but if you want it a
  little spicy, add several drops of hot sauce.)

- Sprinkle with red pepper or paprika and serve with chips.
  Yields 3½ cups.

*Originally Washington State was called "Columbia"
after the Columbia River, but the name was changed to
Washington to avoid confusion with the District of Columbia.*

San Juan Clam Dip

1 (1 ounce) packet onion soup mix
2 (8 ounce) cartons sour cream
1 (7 ounce) can minced clams, drained
3 tablespoons chili sauce
1 tablespoon lemon juice
Assorted crackers

- Combine onion soup mix and sour cream in bowl and mix well.

- Add clams, chili sauce and lemon juice.

- Refrigerate. Serve with assorted crackers. Yields 2 cups.

Simple Salmon Spread

3 ounces cooked smoked salmon
1 (3 ounce) package cream cheese, softened
Juice of 1 lemon
Garlic salt
Seasoned salt

- Beat salmon, cream cheese and a little lemon juice with seasoning to taste in bowl. Serve with crackers. Yields about 1 cup.

What fish can perform operations?
A sturgeon.

Fresh Tomato Salsa

4 medium tomatoes, diced
2 - 4 green onions with tops, diced
1 - 2 jalapeno peppers*
½ cup snipped cilantro leaves
Juice of 1 small lime
1 teaspoon sugar

- Dice tomatoes and onions in large bowl to save juices.

- Wash jalapenos, remove stems and seeds, and dry with paper towels. Dice jalapenos and add to tomato-onion mixture.

- Combine with all other ingredients and 1 teaspoon salt and refrigerate for about 15 to 20 minutes.

- Remove from refrigerator and taste. If tomatoes are too tart, add a little more sugar to cut tartness.

- Refrigerate for about 30 minutes more to blend flavors and serve. Yields 1½ cups.

TIP: Wear rubber gloves when removing seeds from jalapenos.

The Oregon Territory (now Washington and Oregon) was first explored by Bruno Heceta of Spain in 1775, then Captain Robert Gray of America and Captain George Vancouver of Great Britain in 1792 and America's Meriwether Lewis and William Clark in 1805.

Sweet Pepper-Jicama Salsa

5 tomatoes, seeded, chopped
1 bunch green onions with tops, chopped
2 jicama, peeled, chopped
1 red bell pepper, seeded, chopped
1 yellow bell pepper, seeded, chopped
1 green bell pepper, seeded, chopped
1 cucumber, peeled, chopped
2 bunches fresh cilantro, snipped
3 cloves garlic, minced
¼ cup canola oil
¼ cup balsamic vinegar
¼ cup lime juice
1 tablespoon cayenne pepper
1 tablespoon cumin

- Mix tomatoes, onions, jicama, bell peppers and cucumber in large bowl and toss gently.

- In separate bowl, mix cilantro, garlic, canola oil, vinegar, lime juice, cayenne pepper and cumin and blend well.

- Pour over vegetables and toss to coat with dressing. Store in closed container in refrigerator and toss occasionally. Yields 1½ pints.

Washington maintains and operates the largest ferry system in the U.S. and the third largest in the world. The Washington system carries about 25 million people each year. By comparison, the Staten Island Ferry carries about 20 million people annually.

Baked Garlic

2 large heads elephant garlic or 4 - 6 regular heads garlic, peeled
½ cup chicken stock or broth
½ cup white wine
2 tablespoons unsalted butter, melted
Italian bread, sliced

- Preheat oven to 300°.

- Cut off top of garlic heads and discard. Place in small baking dish and pour chicken stock and wine to almost cover garlic.

- Pour melted butter into heads and sprinkle with a little salt and pepper. Bake for 3 hours.

- Remove garlic, break into cloves and squeeze garlic from outer skin. Spread on Italian bread and serve with sauce from baking dish for dipping. Yields 1 cup.

Equivalent measurements for garlic:

1 bulb garlic	*6 to 8 cloves*
2 small cloves garlic	*1 teaspoon minced garlic*
1 large clove garlic	*1½ to 2 teaspoons minced garlic*

Washington state produces 77% of all the hops grown in the U.S. Award-winning fresh hop ales, including ambers, stouts and hefeweizens, are featured annually at the Fresh Hop Ale Festival in Yakima.

Vancouver Garlic-Stuffed Mushrooms

1 tablespoon extra-virgin olive oil
2 tablespoons butter
¾ cup Italian breadcrumbs
3 cloves garlic, peeled, minced
¼ teaspoon oregano
Seasoned salt
Cracked black pepper
18 large mushrooms, stems removed

- Preheat oven to 400°.

- Heat olive oil and butter in skillet over medium heat. Add breadcrumbs, stir to coat and cook for about 5 minutes.

- Add garlic, oregano, seasoned salt and fresh ground black pepper and saute until garlic is translucent.

- Stuff each mushroom with breadcrumb mixture and place in sprayed 9 x 13-inch baking pan. Bake for 20 minutes or until mushrooms are tender. Serve hot or at room temperature. Serves 10 to 12.

Indian tribes in the Columbia Valley area included the Salishan and Shahaptians. Others such as Shoshonees, Athapascans, Kwalhioqua, Nez Perce, Yakima, as well as the Cayuse, Chilluckittequaw, Chimakum, Chinook and Klickitat were all displaced by the influx of settlers from the East.

Sweet Pepper-Garlic Snacks

Olive oil
5 - 6 garlic cloves, peeled
2 (8 ounce) packages cream cheese, softened
¾ cup mayonnaise
**1 (9 ounce) jar roasted sweet red peppers, drained, coarsely
  chopped**
1 bunch fresh green onions with tops, chopped
Red pepper flakes
Chips or crackers

- Preheat oven to 350°.

- Lightly rub a little oil on outside of each garlic clove and place
  in sprayed, shallow baking pan. Heat for about 10 minutes
  and cool.

- Press roasted garlic from outer skins. Beat cream cheese and
  mayonnaise in bowl; stir in garlic, red peppers and onions and
  mix well.

- Sprinkle with red pepper flakes and serve with chips or
  crackers. Serves 4 to 6.

TIP: *Roasted red peppers can be found in jars at the local grocery store.
      They are not hot, but flavorful. If you would like a little spicier dip,
      add several drops of hot sauce or red pepper flakes.*

*According to wikipedia.com, the salmon population in
the Pacific Northwest is less than 3% of what it was at the time of
the Lewis and Clark expedition in 1805.*

Spinach-Feta Pizza

1 tablespoon olive oil
2 cloves garlic, peeled, minced, divided
2 fresh green onions, minced
1 (12 inch) prepared pizza crust
1 (10 ounce) package frozen chopped spinach, thawed
1½ cups shredded mozzarella cheese
8 - 10 grape or cherry tomatoes, halved
1 (4 ounce) can sliced black olives, drained
1 (10 ounce) can green olives, drained, sliced, divided
1 (4 ounce) package crumbled feta cheese

- Preheat oven to 400°.

- Mix oil, 1 clove garlic and green onions in small, microwave-safe bowl and microwave on HIGH for 30 seconds. Prepare pizza crust by rubbing garlic mixture over surface of crust.

- Squeeze spinach between paper towels to completely remove excess moisture. Spread spinach evenly over crust. Sprinkle mozzarella cheese evenly over spinach.

- Add tomato halves, black olives and about half of green olives evenly over cheese. (Save remaining green olives for another use.) Sprinkle with a little salt and pepper and top with feta cheese.

- Bake for about 10 minutes or until cheese melts and crust is golden brown. Let stand 5 minutes before cutting into slices to serve. Serves 2 to 4.

The earliest European to meet natives in the territory was Juan de Fuca, a Greek sailing under the Spanish flag, who visited the straits that now bear his name.

Cheesy Caesar Pizza

1 (12 inch) Italian pizza crust
1 (8 ounce) package shredded mozzarella cheese
1 (6 ounce) package cooked chicken breast strips
2 cups shredded lettuce
3 fresh green onions, sliced
¾ cup shredded cheddar-colby cheese
½ (8 ounce) bottle Caesar dressing

- Preheat oven to 400°.

- Top pizza crust with mozzarella cheese and bake for 8 minutes or until cheese melts.

- Combine chicken strips, lettuce, green onions and cheese in bowl. Pour about half of Caesar dressing over salad and toss.

- Top hot pizza with salad and cut into wedges. Serve immediately. Serves 4 to 6.

The largest metropolitan area in Washington is Seattle.

Before the last ice age, the Columbia River roared over the giant Dry Falls in Washington with 40 times the volume of Niagara Falls. In a 3.5 mile expanse in Coulee City, Washington glacial meltwaters slowly carved out patterns in the 400-foot cliffs.

Baked Brie with Roasted Garlic and Sun-Dried Tomatoes

1 large whole head garlic, peeled
Extra-virgin olive oil
Sprigs of rosemary
1 (12 ounce) round brie cheese
¾ - 1 cup sun-dried tomatoes in oil, drained, chopped
⅓ cup pine nuts
½ cup snipped fresh basil leaves
Crostini

- Preheat oven to 350°.

- Cut about ¼ inch from pointed end of garlic head to expose cloves inside. Place cut end up in foil bowl formed around garlic head.

- Drizzle a little olive oil on top of garlic and drop 2 rosemary sprigs on top. Close foil package loosely. Bake for 45 minutes or until cloves of garlic are tender.

- When garlic cools enough to touch, squeeze garlic out of cloves into small bowl. Stir and spread over round of brie. Arrange tomatoes and pine nuts on top.

- Bake brie for about 15 minutes or until creamy on the inside. Cover top with foil if it begins to brown too much.

- Sprinkle top with basil and serve immediately with crostini or crackers. Serves 8 to 12.

Washington is a diverse geographic region dominated by the Coast Mountains, the Cascades Mountain Range, the Olympic Mountain Range, the Columbia Mountain Range and the Rocky Mountain Range.

Seattle Baked Wontons

½ cup (1 stick) butter, melted, divided
1 (6 ounce) package square wonton skins, halved
1 cup fresh shredded parmesan cheese

- Preheat oven to 400°.

- Brush half of butter on baking sheet and place wonton halves next to each other flat on baking sheet. Spread remaining butter on tops of wontons.

- Spread parmesan generously over wontons and bake until chips begin to brown slightly, about 5 minutes. Serves 4 to 6.

Grilled Tomato-Basil Flatbread

Extra-virgin olive oil
1 (11 ounce) package flatbread
2 large tomatoes, seeded, diced, drained
1 bunch green onions with tops
¼ cup snipped basil leaves
1 cup shredded mozzarella cheese

- Spread light coating of olive oil on both sides of flatbread. Spread tomatoes, onions and basil on top of each flatbread. Cover with cheese.

- Place over low heat on charcoal or gas grill and cook until cheese melts. Break into smaller pieces or serve whole. Serves 4 to 6.

The highest peak in the Pacific Northwest is Mount Rainier in the Washington Cascades at 14,410 feet (4,392 m).

Shrimp Cocktail with Red Sauce

1 cup ketchup
¾ cup chili sauce
2 - 3 tablespoons horseradish sauce
4 - 5 teaspoons lemon juice
1 teaspoon Worcestershire sauce
½ teaspoon hot sauce
1 pound cooked, shelled, veined shrimp

- Mix all ingredients except shrimp in medium bowl. Refrigerate for several hours for flavors to blend.

- Pour into shrimp cocktail serving bowl with sauce in center and shrimp arranged around it.

- If you have a large bowl, fill it with ice before arranging cocktail sauce bowl and shrimp. Serves 2 to 3.

Washington state is ranked as the number one producer in the United States of the following foods.

90% of U.S. production of red raspberries

80% of U.S. production of wrinkled seed peas

75% of U.S. production of hops

73% of U.S. production of spearmint oil

58% of U.S. production of apples

47% of U.S. production of sweet cherries

42% of U.S. production of pears

40% of U.S. production of peppermint oil

39% of U.S. production of concord grapes

36% of U.S. production of carrots grown for processing

Trail Ride Granola

6 cups old-fashioned oats
1½ cups unsweetened coconut
1 cup sliced almonds or pistachios
½ cup crushed wheat germ
½ cup sunflower seeds
½ cup sesame seeds
⅔ cup honey
½ cup canola oil
1 tablespoon vanilla
2 teaspoons ground cinnamon
1 teaspoon ground nutmeg
1 cup raisins

- Preheat oven to 350°.

- Mix oats, coconut, almonds, wheat germ, sunflower seeds and sesame seeds in 9 x 13-inch baking pan.

- Mix honey, oil, vanilla, cinnamon and nutmeg in bowl and pour over granola mix. Stir well to coat all pieces with honey mixture.

- Bake for about 30 minutes. Cool mixture and add raisins. Serves 8 to 10.

Washington is ranked second in the U.S. in the production of lentils, fall potatoes, dry edible peas, asparagus, apricots and sweet corn. And it is ranked third in the production of tart cherries, prunes, plums, summer onions, barley, trout, wheat, cranberries and strawberries.

Mount St. Helens Trail Mix

1 tablespoon canola oil
2 cups old-fashioned oats
⅓ cup packed brown sugar
⅓ cup butter
2 tablespoons honey
⅓ cup dried cranberries
½ cup sliced almonds

- Heat oil in skillet. Add oats and cook over medium heat until oats begin to brown and crisp. Transfer oats to baking sheet.

- Mix brown sugar, butter and honey in same skillet and cook over medium heat, stirring constantly, until bubbly.

- Remove from heat and add oats. Mix well and return all ingredients to baking sheet to cool. Add cranberries and almonds to mixture and store in airtight container after cooling. Serves 8.

TIP: *Add your favorite dried fruits and nuts to the mixture for your own special blend of flavors.*

Since its eruption in 1980, Mount St. Helens is one of America's most famous volcanoes. Coldwater Ridge Visitor Center near Castle Rock, Washington offers great viewing of the volcano.

Coffees, Teas, Punches and Smoothies

Washington Facts

State Bird: *Willow Goldfinch*

State Marine Mammal: *Orca (Killer Whale)*

State Flower: *Coast Rhododendron*

State Fish: *Steelhead Trout*

Emerald City Cafe Latte

1 (12 ounce) can evaporated low-fat milk
2 cups strong, hot, freshly brewed coffee
1 tablespoon sugar

- Pour evaporated milk over coffee in 4-cup measure. Add sugar and microwave on HIGH for 90 seconds. Stir and serve hot or over crushed ice. Serves 2.

Quick Cappuccino

2 cups skim milk or 2% low-fat milk
1 tablespoon sugar
2 cups strong, hot, freshly brewed coffee
Ground cinnamon or nutmeg

- Heat milk and sugar in 4-cup measure in microwave on HIGH for about 2 minutes. Pour into blender and process until frothy.

- Pour hot coffee in mugs and pour froth over top of each. Sprinkle cinnamon or nutmeg on top. Serves 2 to 3.

Smooth Mocha Mudslide

2 cups cafe mocha liquid coffee creamer
2 tablespoons French roast instant coffee granules
2 cups vanilla ice cream or frozen yogurt

- Mix creamer and coffee in blender. Add ice cream and about 3 to 4 cups ice and blend until smooth. Serve cold. Serves 3 to 4.

No matter how old a mother is, she watches her middle-aged children for signs of improvement.

Florida Scott-Maxwell

Black Forest Buzz

1 cup hot brewed coffee
2 tablespoons chocolate syrup
1 tablespoon maraschino cherry juice

- Pour coffee into coffee mug, add chocolate syrup and cherry juice and stir well. Serve hot. Serves 1.

Icy Caramel Coffee

1½ cups brewed coffee, room temperature
½ cup milk
½ cup sugar
2 tablespoons caramel syrup
1 teaspoon chocolate syrup
A few drops vanilla
Ice cubes

- Mix coffee, milk, sugar, caramel syrup, chocolate syrup, vanilla and a pinch of salt in blender container.

- Add about 2 to 3 cups ice cubes and blend until creamy. Serves 2 to 3.

Early Morning Cappuccino Drink

1 packet cappuccino instant breakfast nutritional energy drink
¾ cup milk
⅛ teaspoon ground cinnamon
⅛ teaspoon ground cardamom
½ teaspoon vanilla or almond flavoring

- Mix all ingredients in tall glass and add ice. Serves 1.

Praline Coffee

3 cups hot brewed coffee
¾ cup half-and-half cream
¾ cup packed light brown sugar
2 tablespoons butter
¾ cup praline liqueur
Whipped topping, thawed

- Cook coffee, half-and-half cream, brown sugar and butter in large saucepan over medium heat, stirring constantly. Do not boil. Stir in liqueur.

- Serve coffee with dollop of whipped topping on top. Serves 5 to 6.

Pacific Hot Chocolate

½ cup sugar
¼ cup cocoa powder
4 cups milk
1 teaspoon vanilla

- Mix sugar and cocoa with ⅓ cup water in saucepan over medium heat until sugar and cocoa dissolve and mixture begins to boil.

- Add milk, stirring constantly, and simmer until hot. (Do not boil.)

- Remove from heat, add vanilla and stir briskly with whisk until frothy. Serves 4.

Next time you purchase grapes, place a few clusters in the freezer. When you need a lift, the frozen grapes will pick you right up!

Green Tea Wake-Up

3 cups sparkling ginger ale
¾ cup green tea and honey concentrate
1½ teaspoons honey
4 fresh mint leaves

- Pour ginger ale, green tea and honey concentrate, honey, and mint into pitcher and mix. Pour over ice and serve cold. Serves 4 to 6.

Comfort Chai Tea Mix

2½ cups sugar
2 cups powdered non-dairy creamer
1½ cups unsweetened instant tea
1 cup nonfat dry milk powder
2 teaspoons ground cinnamon
2 teaspoons ground ginger
1 teaspoon ground cardamom
1 teaspoon ground cloves
Vanilla

- Combine all ingredients except vanilla in blender or food processor and process until all ingredients are distributed evenly. Store in airtight jar.

- When ready to serve, pour boiling water into mugs and add ½ to 1 teaspoon vanilla plus 2 heaping tablespoons of chai tea mix for each mug. Serve hot. Yields 3 cups mix.

The major cities of Seattle and Tacoma began as ports supporting the logging, mining, and farming industries of the region, but have developed into major technological and industrial centers which benefit from their location on the Pacific Rim.

Riverfront Orange Tea

12 whole cloves
2 (3 inch) cinnamon sticks, broken
4 tea bags
2 cups no-pulp orange juice
2 tablespoons light brown sugar

- Mix cloves, cinnamon sticks, tea bags and 4 cups water in saucepan and bring to a boil. Remove from heat and let tea stand for about 5 minutes with tea bags. Remove tea bags.

- Pour orange juice and brown sugar into saucepan and heat slightly to dissolve sugar. Remove from heat and pour into pitcher to serve. Tea may be served hot or cold. Serves 6 to 8.

Strawberry Punch

2 (10 ounce) boxes frozen strawberries, thawed
2 (6 ounce) cans frozen pink lemonade concentrate
2 (2 liter) bottles ginger ale, chilled

- Process strawberries through blender. Pour lemonade into punch bowl and stir in strawberries.

- Add chilled ginger ale and stir well. (It would be nice to make an ice ring with another bottle of ginger ale.) Serves 24.

If you need a quick festive punch or a special, celebratory drink, champagne and canned fruit juices can save the day. Choose tropical flavors or bright colors. Mix two parts champagne and one or two parts juice and you have a beautiful, delightful drink in just a few minutes.

Sparkling Cranberry Punch

Ice mold for punch bowl
Red food coloring
2 quarts cranberry juice cocktail
1 (6 ounce) can frozen lemonade, thawed
1 quart ginger ale, chilled

- Pour water in mold for ice ring and add red food coloring to make mold brighter and prettier.

- Mix cranberry juice and lemonade in pitcher. Refrigerate until ready to serve.

- When ready to serve, pour cranberry mixture into punch bowl, add ginger ale and stir well.

- Add decorative ice mold to punch bowl. Serves 24.

Mulled Hot Apple Cider

2 quarts apple cider or apple juice
2 teaspoons whole cloves
2 teaspoons whole allspice
6 sticks cinnamon

- Combine all ingredients in large saucepan. Heat for 15 to 20 minutes over low heat; remove whole cloves, allspice and cinnamon sticks and serve immediately. Serves 8 to 10.

To slow down discoloration in slices of light-colored fruits, spritz with lemon juice or dip in a solution of 1 quart water and 1 tablespoon lemon juice.

Washington State Apple Cider

1 (32 ounce) bottle apple cider
½ cup maple syrup
½ cup (1 stick) butter
¼ cup packed brown sugar
½ teaspoon ground cinnamon
½ teaspoon ground nutmeg

- Cook apple cider and maple syrup in large saucepan or slow cooker long enough for syrup to dissolve and stir occasionally.

- Combine butter, brown sugar, cinnamon and nutmeg in bowl. Pour apple cider into mugs, top with spoonful of butter-cinnamon mixture and stir. Serve hot. Serves 6 to 8.

Easy Breezy Strawberry Smoothie

½ cup fresh strawberries, sliced
½ cup skim milk
2 teaspoons sugar or ⅛ teaspoon stevia

- Combine strawberries, milk and sugar in blender. Blend until smooth and creamy. Serves 1..

TIP: *To make thicker shake, add 3 ice cubes to blender. Also, you can substitute frozen, unsweetened berries for fresh ones.*

For a quick, easy, refreshing summer beverage, mix citrus juices with fresh berries of your choice and serve chilled. (Halve berries if they are large.)

Berry-Carrot Juicer

½ cup apple juice, chilled
½ cup low-fat milk
8 baby carrots
1 cup frozen mixed berries

- Place all ingredients in blender with 1 to 2 cups ice cubes and process until creamy. Serves 1.

Berry Special Smoothie

1½ cups milk
1 (8 ounce) carton blueberry yogurt
1 teaspoon instant lemonade mix
1 cup blueberries

- Combine milk, yogurt and lemonade mix and whip slightly in blender. Add blueberries and process until smooth. Serves 3 to 4.

Chocolate-Banana Smoothie

1 cup milk
1 banana
1 tablespoon chocolate syrup

- Combine all ingredients to blender and process with crushed ice until slushy. Serves 1.

TIP: For a creamier texture, substitute ice cream or frozen yogurt for milk.

Go-Grapeberry Smoothie

2 pink grapefruit
1 cup chopped ripe mango
1 medium banana
1 (8 ounce) carton strawberry-banana yogurt
2 tablespoons honey
½ teaspoon white vanilla

- Slice grapefruit into halves and squeeze enough fresh juice to equal 1⅓ cups.

- Pour juice into blender and add mango, banana, strawberry-banana yogurt, honey, vanilla and about ½ cup ice.

- Blend and process several times. Add additional ½ cup ice and process until smooth. Serves 4 to 6.

After the Mississippi, more water flows through the Columbia than any other river in the lower 48 states.

Friday Harbor in Washington's San Juan Islands is home to the Whale Museum.

Breakfast, Brunch and Breads

Washington Facts

State Insect:	*Green Darter Dragonfly*
State Fossil:	*Columbian Mammoth*
State Gem:	*Petrified Wood*
State Endemic Mammal:	*Olympic Marmot*

Coffee Lover's Coffee Cake

2 cups flour
2 teaspoons instant coffee granules
2 cups packed brown sugar
1 teaspoon ground cinnamon
½ cup (1 stick) butter
1 (8 ounce) carton sour cream
1 teaspoon baking soda
1 egg
¾ cup chopped pecans

- Preheat oven to 350°.

- Combine flour, instant coffee, brown sugar, ½ teaspoon salt and cinnamon in bowl and stir well.

- Cut in butter until crumbly. Press half of mixture into sprayed 9-inch square pan.

- In separate bowl, combine sour cream, baking soda and egg and mix well. Add to remaining crumb mixture and stir until dry ingredients are moist.

- Pour mixture over crumb crust in pan. Sprinkle with pecans. Bake for 45 to 60 minutes. Serves 8 to 10.

Seafair is Seattle, Washington's annual event celebrating the community spirit of Puget Sound residents. Seafair began in 1950 to commemorate the city's centennial.

Yakima Apple Bake

1 (8 ounce) can refrigerated crescent dinner rolls
3 tablespoons plus ½ cup sugar, divided
2 teaspoons ground cinnamon, divided
1 apple, peeled, cored
½ cup whipping cream
1 tablespoon almond extract
1 egg, beaten
½ cup sliced almonds

- Preheat oven to 375°.

- Separate crescent dinner rolls and place on sprayed baking
  sheet. Flatten each roll into 8 triangles, but do not let
  them touch.

- Mix 3 tablespoons sugar and 1 teaspoon cinnamon in small
  bowl. Sprinkle mixture over each triangle and pat into dough.

- Cut apple into 8 slices and place each slice on wide end of
  triangle. Wrap sides on left and right over apple and roll
  starting with wide end. Press and seal seams.

- Place each triangle seam-side down around 9-inch round
  baking dish with 1 in middle. Bake for 15 to 20 minutes.

- Mix ½ cup sugar, whipping cream, almond extract and egg in
  bowl with whisk until ingredients blend well.

- Drizzle mixture evenly over partially cooked coffee cake.
  Sprinkle almonds and remaining 1 teaspoon cinnamon
  over top.

- Bake for additional 14 to 15 minutes or until cake is golden
  brown. If necessary, cover pan with foil during last 5 minutes
  of baking time to prevent excessive browning. Serve warm.
  Serves 8.

Wenatchee Fried Apples

⅓ cup butter
⅓ cup packed brown sugar
2 tablespoons lemon juice
6 Washington State red delicious apples, peeled, cored, sliced

- Mix butter, brown sugar, lemon juice and ¼ cup water in large saucepan. Add apple slices, cover and cook over medium heat until tender. Stir frequently to prevent sticking. Do not burn.

- Remove from heat and set aside for about 10 minutes before serving. Serves 6.

Breakfast Fruit Bowl

Red huckleberries in Washington are always called huckleberries, but other species may be called blueberries or huckleberries depending on local custom. Huckleberries can be found in the Pacific Northwest on the lower slopes of mountains.

1 cup flavored or plain yogurt
1 tablespoon honey
½ cup granola cereal
2 cups fresh pear slices or huckleberries

- Mix yogurt and honey with granola in bowl and top with fruit slices. Make as individual servings in bowls or mix together and serve. Serves 4.

The majority of Washington's apple crop comes from two areas: Wenatchee-Okanogan area including Chelan, Okanogan, Douglas and Grant counties; and the Yakima region including Yakima, Benton and Kittitas counties.

Blackberry-Brie Brunch Flip

1 (6 ounce) package blackberries
4 eggs
2 tablespoons milk
1 tablespoon plus 1 teaspoon butter, divided
1 (4 ounce) block brie, trimmed, cubed

- Place 1 teaspoon butter in skillet and heat on medium-high. Beat eggs with milk and pour half of mixture into skillet. As eggs cook, tilt skillet to pour uncooked part of eggs into skillet.

- When eggs are almost done, place half brie and half blackberries on half of eggs. Carefully flip other half of eggs over to cover brie and blackberries.

- Cook 30 seconds or so until brie melts slightly, remove from skillet and serve immediately.

- Repeat process for second omelet. Serves 2.

Washington produces a wide variety of agricultural products because of the various climate zones in the state.

- *The maritime climate zone keeps the western, coastal part of the state cool in the summer and warm in the winter. The average rainfall in the lower areas is about 40 inches per year.*

- *A temperate rain forest exists in the Cascade Mountains where rainfall is about 140 inches per year.*

- *The Cascades block much of the coastal moisture from getting to the eastern part of the state where there is a steppe climate zone with rainfall of about 10 to 20 inches.*

- *In central Washington there is a desert climate zone where rainfall is less than 10 inches per year. The Grand Coulee Dam, built in 1941 for irrigation usage, enables the Columbia Basin area to be used as farmland.*

Avocado-Stuffed Omelet

8 large eggs
½ cup milk
1 avocado, seeded, peeled, diced
¾ cup shredded Monterey Jack cheese
¾ cup seeded, minced, drained tomatoes
½ cup minced green onions with tops

- Beat eggs with milk vigorously in bowl. Pour into large, sprayed skillet. Cook over low heat until eggs begin to firm up. Slide eggs around in skillet while cooking.

- Mix avocado, cheese, tomatoes and onions in bowl and spread over one-half of eggs. Use spatula to lift other half of eggs onto cheese mixture. Cook until firm on the inside and cheese melts. Serves 4 to 6.

More than 175,000 acres of apple orchards are located in the foothills of the Cascade Mountains. An estimated 40,000 pickers harvest the crop from August to November.

Washington State apple orchards include the Red and Golden Delicious, Granny Smith, Braeburn, Jonagold, Fuji, Gala and many other varieties.

Kennewick Asparagus Quiche

1 (9 inch) frozen piecrust
¼ cup (½ stick) butter
3 tablespoons flour
1½ cups milk
4 eggs
1 pound fresh asparagus, trimmed, chopped
½ cup shredded Swiss cheese
¼ cup breadcrumbs

- Preheat oven to 450°.

- Place several sheets of heavy-duty foil in piecrust and over edge. Bake for about 5 minutes. Remove from oven, discard foil and bake for additional 5 minutes.

- Melt butter in saucepan and stir in flour and a little salt. Stir to dissolve all lumps. Cook over medium heat and gradually pour in milk. Continue to stir until mixture thickens.

- Add remaining ingredients except breadcrumbs and heat. Pour into piecrust and sprinkle breadcrumbs over quiche.

- Bake for about 30 minutes or until knife inserted in center comes out clean. Cool slightly, slice into wedges and serve warm. Serves 6.

"Asparagus, next to orange juice, is regarded as the second best whole food source of folic acid. Folic acid is known to lower the risk of heart disease, colon cancer, liver disease and spina bifida." The Washington Asparagus Commission

Smoked Salmon Breakfast Tacos

1 medium onion, chopped
1 teaspoon canola oil
3 eggs
2 (3.75 ounce) cans red salmon, drained, flaked
½ teaspoon hot sauce
12 flour tortillas
1 (8 ounce) package shredded cheese
2 cups shredded cabbage

- Saute onions in oil in skillet until onions are translucent. Beat eggs in bowl and add to onions.

- Scramble eggs and cook over medium heat. Add salmon and hot sauce and cook until eggs are firm. Stir often.

- Heat tortillas in oven or microwave wrapped in slightly damp paper towels.

- Spread egg mixture equally on tortillas. Add cheese and cabbage, roll and serve immediately. Serves 4.

Salmon is considered a relatively healthy food because it contains high protein, low fat levels and has high Omega-3 fatty acids; on the negative side it also contains cholesterol.

The Columbia River receives drainage from seven states: Oregon, Washington, Idaho, Montana, Nevada, Wyoming and Utah and one Canadian province. The river runs 1,200 miles from the base of the Canadian Rockies in southeastern British Columbia to the Pacific Ocean at Astoria, Oregon and Ilwaco, Washington.

Applesauce-Pecan Bread

1 cup sugar
1 cup applesauce
⅓ cup canola oil
2 eggs
2 tablespoons milk
1 teaspoon almond extract
2 cups flour
1 teaspoon baking soda
½ teaspoon baking powder
¾ teaspoon ground cinnamon
¼ teaspoon ground nutmeg
¾ cup chopped pecans

- Preheat oven to 350°.
- Combine sugar, applesauce, oil, eggs, milk and almond extract in bowl and mix well.
- Combine all dry ingredients and ¼ teaspoon salt; add to sugar mixture and mix well. Fold in pecans. Pour into sprayed, floured 9 x 5-inch loaf pan.

Topping:

½ cup chopped pecans
½ teaspoon ground cinnamon
½ cup packed brown sugar

- Combine pecans, cinnamon and brown sugar in bowl. Sprinkle over batter.
- Bake for 1 hour 5 minutes. Bread is done when toothpick inserted in center comes out clean. Cool on rack. Serves 12.

Banana-Pineapple Loaf

This is wonderful sliced, buttered and toasted for breakfast.

1 cup (2 sticks) butter, softened
1 cup sugar
4 eggs
1 cup mashed ripe bananas
4 cups sifted flour
2 teaspoons baking powder
1 teaspoon baking soda
1 (15 ounce) can crushed pineapple with juice
1 (7 ounce) can flaked coconut
1 cup chopped pecans

- Preheat oven to 350°.

- Cream butter and sugar in bowl, add eggs and mix well. Stir in bananas.

- In separate bowl, sift flour, baking powder, baking soda and ½ teaspoon salt and add to butter mixture. Fold in pineapple, coconut and pecans.

- Pour into 2 sprayed, floured 9 x 5-inch loaf pans. Bake for 1 hour 10 minutes. Bread is done when toothpick inserted in center comes out clean. Serves 12 to 16.

TIP: For lunch, spread cream cheese on slices of banana-pineapple bread, cut into thirds and serve as finger sandwiches. (Remove crusts for the ladies.)

Cascades National Park Service Complex in Washington includes North Cascades National Park and Ross Lake and Lake Chelan National Recreation Areas. Lake Chelan is one of America's deepest lakes at 1,500 feet.

Old Pioneer Pumpkin Bread

*This is fabulous served with lots of butter or for
sandwiches with cream cheese filling.*

1 cup canola oil
3 cups sugar
4 eggs
1 teaspoon vanilla
1 (15 ounce) can pumpkin
2 teaspoons baking soda
2 teaspoons ground cinnamon
¼ teaspoon ground allspice
3 cups flour
1 cup chopped dates
1½ - 2 cups chopped pecans

- Preheat oven to 350°.

- Combine oil and sugar in bowl; add eggs one at a time and beat
  well after each addition. Add vanilla and pumpkin and
  mix well.

- In separate bowl, sift 1 teaspoon salt, baking soda, cinnamon,
  allspice and flour. Add to sugar-pumpkin mixture and beat
  well. Stir in dates and pecans.

- Pour into 2 large sprayed, floured 9 x 5-inch loaf pans.

- Bake for 1 hour 10 minutes to 1 hour 15 minutes. Bread is
  done when toothpick inserted in center comes out clean.
  Serves 12 to 16.

*Lake Roosevelt National Recreation Area in
Washington was created when Grand Coulee Dam was built
on the Columbia River. Completed in 1942; it created Lake
Roosevelt, a 130-mile-long lake.*

Very Berry Strawberry Bread

3 cups sifted flour
2 cups sugar
1 teaspoon baking soda
1 tablespoon ground cinnamon
3 large eggs, beaten
1 cup canola oil
1¼ cups chopped walnuts
2 (10 ounce) packages frozen sweetened strawberries with juice,
   thawed
1 (8 ounce) package light cream cheese, softened

- Preheat oven to 350°.

- Combine flour, sugar, 1 teaspoon salt, baking soda and cinnamon in large bowl. Add remaining ingredients except cream cheese.

- Pour in 2 sprayed, floured 9 x 5-inch loaf pans.

- Bake for 1 hour or when toothpick inserted in center comes out clean. Cool for several minutes before removing from pan.

- To serve, slice bread and spread cream cheese between 2 slices. For finger sandwiches, cut in smaller pieces. Serves 12 to 16.

It is best to wash fresh berries just before eating them. They will keep better if stored in an airtight container with a layer of paper towels in the bottom.

Zucchini-Pineapple Bread

3 eggs, beaten
2 cups sugar
1 cup canola oil
2 teaspoons vanilla
2 cups grated zucchini
3 cups flour
1 teaspoon baking soda
1 tablespoon ground cinnamon
½ teaspoon baking powder
1 cup chopped pecans
1 (8 ounce) can crushed pineapple, drained
1 (8 ounce) carton cream cheese, softened

- Preheat oven to 325°.

- Mix eggs, sugar, oil and vanilla in bowl and mix well.

- Add remaining ingredients except cream cheese. Add
  1 teaspoon salt, mix well and pour in 2 sprayed, floured
  9 x 5-inch loaf pans.

- Bake for 60 minutes or until toothpick inserted in center comes
  out clean. Cool for several minutes.

- To serve, slice and spread with cream cheese. Serves 12 to 16.

*Washington's Mount Rainier National Park has
excellent examples of old growth forest and sub-alpine meadows.
More than 2 million people visit each year.*

Jingle Bread

Yes, the sausage is right in the bread! A slice or two,
warmed or toasted makes a great breakfast!

¾ cup raisins
1 pound hot ground sausage
1½ cups packed light brown sugar
1½ cups sugar
2 eggs
1 cup chopped pecans
3 cups flour
1 teaspoon ground ginger
1 teaspoon ground allspice
1 teaspoon ground cinnamon
1 teaspoon baking powder
1 teaspoon baking soda
1 cup cold brewed coffee

- Preheat oven to 350°.

- Cover raisins with water in saucepan, simmer for 5 minutes and drain.

- Combine uncooked sausage, brown sugar, sugar and eggs in bowl and stir in pecans and raisins.

- In separate bowl, combine flour, ginger, allspice, cinnamon and baking powder.

- In separate bowl, stir baking soda into coffee, blend coffee into flour mixture and stir all into sausage mixture. (This is when you have fun mixing with your hands.)

- Pour into 2 sprayed, floured loaf pans. Bake for 1 hour 10 minutes or until toothpick inserted in center comes out clean. Refrigerate. Serves 20.

Fireside Bread

1 loaf French bread
½ cup (1 stick) butter, softened
2 teaspoons chopped onion
1 teaspoon dry mustard
2 teaspoons celery seed
½ cup shredded mozzarella or Swiss cheese

- Preheat oven to 350°.

- Peel top and sides of crust from French bread. Slice bread into 2-inch slices, but not all the way through.

- Combine butter, onion, mustard and celery seed in small bowl. Spread mixture between slices of bread but set aside 3 tablespoons.

- Spread rest of butter mixture on top and sides of bread. Sprinkle cheese over top. Wrap in foil and leave top of bread uncovered.

- Bake until top is light brown. Serves 8 to 10.

Washington State produces more apples than any other state.

Great Britian ceded its claims to the Pacific Northwest to the U.S. in the Treaty of Oregon in 1846. The area was called the Oregon Territory and included Oregon, Washington, Idaho and parts of Montana. Washington gained statehood in 1889.

Apple-Spice Muffins

1 cup (2 sticks) butter, softened
1 cup packed brown sugar
1 cup sugar
2 eggs
1¾ cups applesauce
2 teaspoons ground cinnamon
1 teaspoon ground allspice
½ teaspoon ground cloves
2 teaspoons baking soda
3½ cups flour
1½ cups chopped pecans

- Preheat oven to 375°.

- Cream butter, brown sugar and sugar in bowl.

- Add eggs, applesauce, cinnamon, allspice, cloves, ½ teaspoon salt, baking soda and flour and mix well. Add pecans and stir well.

- Pour into 28 sprayed muffin cups (or use paper liners). Bake for 16 minutes. Serves 28.

Ginger-Raisin Muffins

1 (18 ounce) box gingerbread mix
1 egg
2 (1.5 ounce) boxes seedless raisins

- Preheat oven to 350°.

- Combine gingerbread mix, 1¼ cups lukewarm water and egg in bowl and mix well. Stir in raisins.

- Fill sprayed muffin cups half full.

- Bake for 20 minutes or when toothpick inserted in center comes out clean. Serves 16.

Pear Muffins

1 cup flour
1 cup whole wheat flour
⅓ cup packed brown sugar
2½ teaspoons baking powder
½ teaspoon baking soda
½ teaspoon ground ginger
¼ teaspoon ground allspice
¾ cup buttermilk*
⅓ cup canola oil
1 egg, beaten
1 large pear

- Preheat oven to 400°.

- Mix flour, whole wheat flour, brown sugar, baking powder, baking soda, ginger, allspice and ¼ teaspoon salt in large bowl.

- In separate bowl, mix buttermilk, oil and egg. Gradually pour into flour mixture and fold gently.

- Peel, core and shred pear and add to batter. Pour into 12 sprayed muffin cups and bake for about 20 minutes. Yields 12 muffins.

*TIP: To make buttermilk, mix 1 cup milk with 1 tablespoon lemon juice or vinegar and let milk stand for about 10 minutes.

The Pacific Northwest, including Washington, Oregon and northern California, accounts for 98% of the total pear production in the U.S. Washington is the leading producer of pears in the U.S.

Apple Fritters

½ cup milk
2 eggs
1 cup flour
3 tablespoons sugar
¼ teaspoon ground cinnamon
1½ cups peeled, cored, chopped apples
Canola oil
Powdered sugar
Maple syrup

- Beat milk and eggs in small bowl.

- In separate bowl, mix flour, sugar, cinnamon and a pinch of salt. Pour milk mixture into flour and stir well. Mix in apples.

- Heat oil to 365°. Drop batter by spoonfuls into hot oil. Fry until golden brown. Remove from hot oil and drain on paper towel.

- Before serving, sprinkle with powdered sugar. Serve with maple syrup. Serves 8 to 10.

A 2008 study by Victor Fulgoni, PhD, found that apples are one of the foods that most decreases the risk of death from both coronary heart disease and cardiovascular disease among post-menopausal women. Pectin, fiber found in apples, builds up in the digestive tract to lower cholesterol levels and decrease the risk of heart attack and stroke.

Pear Fritters

½ cup milk
2 eggs
1 cup flour
3 tablespoons sugar
¼ teaspoon ground nutmeg
1½ cups peeled, cored, chopped pears
Canola oil
Powdered sugar
Maple syrup

- Beat milk and eggs in small bowl.

- In separate bowl, mix flour, sugar, nutmeg and a pinch of salt. Pour milk mixture into flour and stir well. Mix in pears.

- Heat oil to 365°. Drop batter by spoonfuls into hot oil. Fry until golden brown.

- Remove from hot oil and drain on paper towel.

- Before serving, sprinkle with powdered sugar. Serve with maple syrup. Serves 8 to 10.

The San Juan Islands National Historical Park in Washington was designated as a World Cultural Heritage site in 1983. The site included forts, bastions and powder houses. Sections of the sandstone walls built in the 1630's still remain.

Apple-Cider Syrup

This is great over pancakes.

1 cup apple cider or apple juice
1 tablespoon cornstarch
½ cup sugar
1 tablespoon lemon juice
1 teaspoon ground cinnamon
½ teaspoon vanilla
2 tablespoons butter

- Combine apple cider and cornstarch in saucepan; stir continuously and cook over medium heat for several minutes.

- Continue stirring, reduce heat and add sugar, lemon juice, cinnamon and vanilla. Cook for about 3 to 4 minutes and remove from heat.

- Add butter and stir. Pour over waffles or pancakes while hot. Yields 1½ cups.

The Washington Apple Commission has a great tip for shoppers. Always choose apples that have shiny skins. Skins that are dull will not be crisp and tasty.

Bartlett pears are good for jams and jellies and are one of the best varieties to eat raw.

Pear Preserves

Pears
6 cups sugar
Ball® Fruit-Fresh®
1 lemon

- Peel, core and cut enough pears into small slices to equal 1 gallon or 16 cups. Sprinkle sugar and Fruit-Fresh over pears, cover and set aside overnight.

- Bring pears to a boil in large pot. Add 2 small slices lemon peel and cook very slowly until pears are clear and amber-colored and syrup is thick, about 2 hours.

- Sterilize jars and lids in barely boiling water. Lift jar from hot water with tongs. Pack preserves into hot jar and wipe rims of jars with cloth. Place lid and ring on jar and tighten.

- Turn upside down on cabinet top and leave until cool. When cool, check lid for successful seal. Press middle of lid. If it springs up when released, the lid is not sealed. Refrigerate unsealed jars to prevent spoilage. Yields 4 pints.

Pears in the grocery store are usually green and hard because they ripen better off the tree. The best way for them to ripen is to be stored in a paper bag at room temperature until the flesh at the neck gives a little when you press against it. Once ripe they should be stored in the coldest part of the refrigerator.

Food Festivals in Washington

Month	Name	Place
February	Chocolate Extravaganza	Cathlamet
February	Chocolate on the Beach Fest	Pacific Beach
March	Penn Cove Mussel Festival	Whidbey Island
March	Crab & Oyster Feed	Rosburg
March	Razor Clam Festival	Ocean Shores
March	Sharon Grange Oyster Feed	Porter
April	World Class Crab Races & Crab Feed	Westport
May	Cheese Festival	Seattle
May	Manson Apple Blossom Festival	Manson
May	Oyster Feed	Ocosta
May	Willapa Bay Seafood Fest	Nahcotta
June	Bellevue Strawberry Fest	Bellevue
June	Berry Dairy Days	Burlington
June	Northwest Garlic Festival	Ocean Park
July	Ballard Seafood Fest	Ballard
July	Hoike and Hawaiian Fest	Vancouver
July	Raspberry Fest	Lynden
July	Seattle Seafair	Seattle
July	Walla Walla Sweet Onion Fest	Walla Walla
August	Brady's World Famous Oyster Feed	Westport
August	Garlic Festival	Chehalis
August	National Lentil Festival	Pullman
August	Westport Seafood Festival	Westport
September	Annual Seafood Festival	Westport
September	Buzzard's Breath Chili Cook-Off	Cathlamet
September	Burlington Harvest Festival & Pumpkin Pitch	Burlington
September	Coffee Fest Seattle	Seattle
September	Commencement Bay Maritime Festival	Tacoma
September	Grapefest	Kennewick
September	Huckleberry Festival	Bingen
September	Pasco's Fiery Foods Festival	Pasco
September	Wenatchee River Salmon Festival	Leavenworth
September	Zucchini Fest	Oakville
October	Apple Festival at the Big Red Barn	Yakima
October	Cranberry Harvest Festival	Grayland
October	Dungeness Crab & Seafood Festival	Port Angeles
October	Everett Sausage Fest	Everett
October	Harvest Fest	Lynden
October	Issaquah Salmon Days Festival	Issaquah
October	OysterFest	Shelton
October	Wild Mushroom Festival	Long Beach

Salads
and
Soups

Washington Facts

State Highest Point: *Mount Rainier (14,410 feet)*

State Largest City: *Seattle*

State Capital: *Olympia*

State Tree: *Western Hemlock*

Major Rivers: *Columbia, Snake, Yakima*

Cherry-Pecan Gelatin Mold

1 (8 ounce) can pitted black bing cherries
1 (6 ounce) package cherry gelatin
½ cup chopped pecans
1 cup whipping cream, whipped

- Drain cherries, save juice and chop cherries. Pour juice into measuring cup and add enough water to make 2 cups liquid. Dissolve gelatin into 1 cup boiling water in bowl and stir until completely clear. Stir in cherry juice and allow to cool.

- Refrigerate just until it starts to set, then fold in cherries, pecans and whipped cream. Turn into sprayed mold and refrigerate overnight.

- To serve, run a knife around edge of mold to let in air, then invert onto serving plate. Serves 8 to 10.

Cherry Salad Fluff

This works as a dessert too.

1 (14 ounce) can fat-free sweetened condensed milk
1 (8 ounce) can crushed pineapple, drained
¼ cup lemon juice
1 (20 ounce) can lite cherry pie filling
1 (12 ounce) carton whipped topping, thawed

- Mix sweetened condensed milk, pineapple and lemon juice in bowl. Add pie filling and whipped topping. Refrigerate until firm. Serves 16.

Most of the population in the Pacific Northwest is concentrated in the Vancouver-Seattle-Portland corridor.

Grilled Grapefruit Cups

3 pink or ruby red grapefruit
2 white grapefruit
4 oranges
2 limes
½ cup sherry
¼ cup plus 1 tablespoon packed light brown sugar
3 tablespoons butter

- Cut grapefruit in half, remove interior flesh over large bowl and divide fruit into sections. Save juices in bowl with fruit and set grapefruit shells aside.

- Cut top and bottom from oranges and limes over same bowl and discard them. Cut between pulp and inside peel and remove fruit. Remove any white portions on outside of fruit. Divide into sections and mix with grapefruit in bowl. Discard peels.

- Drain juices from fruit bowl and set aside. Pour sherry over fruit, cover and marinate for 1 hour in refrigerator.

- Place mixed fruit in grapefruit shells and sprinkle brown sugar over fruit. Divide butter equally among fruit in grapefruit shells. Place in 9 x 13-inch baking dish and broil in oven until butter melts and sugar crystallizes.

- Pour remaining juices over top and serve immediately. Serves 6.

The Oregon Coast, the Columbia River and Columbia River Gorge National Scenic Area, Mount St. Helens and Hells Canyon National Recreation Area on the Snake River are among the many diverse and beautiful natural features in Oregon and Washington.

Curried Fruit Medley

1 (29 ounce) can sliced peaches
2 (15 ounce) cans pineapple chunks
1 (10 ounce) jar maraschino cherries
1 cup packed brown sugar
1 teaspoon curry powder
¼ cup (½ stick) butter, cut into pieces

- Preheat oven to 350°.

- Drain fruit and place in 9 x 13-inch baking dish.

- Combine brown sugar and curry powder in bowl and stir well. Sprinkle over fruit and dot with butter.

- Cover and bake for 30 minutes or until thoroughly hot. Serves 8.

Avocado-Spinach Salad

2 ripe avocados
1 (5 ounce) package baby spinach
½ (16 ounce) carton grape tomatoes, halved
1 (4 ounce) package crumbled feta cheese
1 small red onion, chopped
⅓ cup coarsely chopped pistachios
Freshly ground peppercorns

- Just before serving, peel, slice and cube avocados. Mix with remaining ingredients in bowl except dressing. Serve your favorite dressing on the side. Serves 4.

Vancouver Island has one of the world's most diverse ecosystems encompassing rain forests, marshes, meadows, beaches, mountains, ocean, rivers and lakes.

Bellingham Broccoli-Noodle Salad

1 cup slivered almonds, toasted
1 cup sunflower seeds, toasted
2 (3 ounce) packages chicken-flavored ramen noodles
1 (16 ounce) package broccoli slaw
1 (8 ounce) bottle Italian salad dressing

- Preheat oven to 255°.

- Toast almonds and sunflower seeds on baking sheet for about
  10 minutes. Break up ramen noodles and mix with slaw,
  almonds and sunflower seeds in bowl.

- Toss with Italian salad dressing and refrigerate. Serves 12 to 16.

Crunchy Cauliflower-Broccoli Salad

1 head cauliflower, cut into florets
1 bunch broccoli, cut into florets
1 cup mayonnaise
¾ cup sour cream
1 tablespoon white wine vinegar
1 tablespoon sugar
½ teaspoon hot sauce
1 onion, chopped

- After washing cauliflower and broccoli, allow vegetables to
  stand so they will completely drain.

- Mix mayonnaise, sour cream, vinegar, sugar, hot sauce, onion,
  1 teaspoon salt and ½ teaspoon pepper in bowl.

- Pour dressing over vegetables and toss. Refrigerate for several
  hours before serving. Serves 8 to 10.

Parslied Potato Salad

2 pounds new (red) potatoes, quartered
¾ - 1 cup Caesar dressing
½ cup grated parmesan cheese
¼ cup chopped fresh parsley
½ cup chopped roasted red peppers

- Cook potatoes in saucepan in boiling water until fork-tender and drain.

- Place potatoes in large bowl and pour dressing over them.

- Add cheese, parsley and red peppers and toss lightly. Serve warm or chilled. Serves 6 to 8.

Nutty Zucchini Salad

6 cups torn mixed salad greens
1 medium zucchini, sliced
1 (8 ounce) can sliced water chestnuts, drained
½ cup peanuts
⅓ cup Italian salad dressing

- Toss greens, zucchini, water chestnuts and peanuts in bowl.

- When ready to serve, add salad dressing and toss. Serves 6.

More than 200,000 people attend the annual Issaquah Salmon Days Festival in early October. The festival coincides with the arrival of Pacific salmon in Issaquah Creek in Washington, the destination point of their 40-mile trip from Puget Sound.

Northwest Chinese Salad

¾ cup slivered almonds
2 (3 ounce) packages chicken-flavored ramen noodles,
    broken in pieces
6 tablespoons (¾ stick) butter
1 head cabbage, shredded
5 green onions with tops, chopped
½ cup sunflower seeds

- Brown almonds and noodles in butter in skillet over low heat. Mix in with shredded cabbage, green onions and sunflower seeds.

Dressing:

1 cup olive oil
3 teaspoons soy sauce
1 cup sugar
½ cup vinegar

- Mix oil, soy sauce, sugar, vinegar and a little salt in bowl. Add to salad when ready to serve. Serves 8.

Early Belgian and French colonists brought the first pear trees to America's eastern coast, but crop blights proved too severe for widespread cultivation. The same pear trees were carried overland to the Oregon Territory and met with much more success. The pear varieties planted by the first colonists and prized for their delicate flavor and buttery taste are still grown today and are some of the best in the world. Washington leads the United States in pear production.

Korean Spinach Salad

1 (10 ounce) package spinach, washed, drained, torn in pieces
1 (14 ounce) can bean sprouts, drained
8 slices cooked crisp bacon, crumbled
3 eggs, hard-boiled, sliced

- Pat spinach and sprouts lightly with paper towels. Toss spinach, bean sprouts, bacon and eggs gently in bowl.

Dressing:

1 cup olive oil
⅓ cup ketchup
½ cup sugar
½ cup red wine vinegar
1 tablespoon Worcestershire sauce
1 medium onion, chopped

- Whisk olive oil, ketchup, sugar, vinegar, Worcestershire sauce, onion, and a little salt and pepper vigorously in bowl and serve beside the salad. Serves 8.

Terrific Tortellini Salad

2 (14 ounce) packages frozen cheese tortellini
1 green bell pepper, seeded, diced
1 red bell pepper, seeded, diced
1 cucumber, chopped, drained
1 (14 ounce) can artichoke hearts, rinsed, halved, drained
1 (8 ounce) bottle creamy Caesar salad dressing

- Prepare tortellini according to package directions and drain. Rinse with cold water, drain and refrigerate.

- Combine tortellini, bell peppers, cucumber, artichoke hearts and dressing in large bowl. Cover and refrigerate for at least 2 hours before serving. Serves 8 to 10.

Olympia Spring Greens Salad

1 (5 ounce) package fresh spring greens salad mix
¾ cup quartered strawberries, drained
⅓ cup pistachios, coarsely chopped
⅓ cup raisins
1 large ripe avocado
Lemon juice
⅓ cup blue cheese crumbles
Raspberry dressing

- Toss spring greens, strawberries, pistachios and raisins in bowl gently and refrigerate.

- Just before serving, peel and slice avocado. Sprinkle a little lemon juice over slices. Sprinkle blue cheese crumbles and avocado on top. Serve dressing with salad. Serves 4.

Picture Lake Red Salad

4 cups torn mixed salad greens
3 fresh green onions with tops, chopped
2 medium red apples with peels, diced
1 cup fresh raspberries or huckleberries
½ cup poppy seed dressing

- Toss salad greens, green onions and fruit in bowl.

- Drizzle with dressing and toss. Serves 4 to 6.

The temperate rain forests in the Pacific Northwest are among the rainiest places in the world.

Chinese Chicken Salad

2 cups cooked, chopped chicken
1 cup diced celery
1 (11 ounce) can mandarin oranges, drained
⅓ cup sliced almonds, toasted
¾ cup whipped topping, thawed
¾ cup Catalina dressing
1 cup chow mein noodles

- Mix chicken, celery, mandarin oranges and almonds in large bowl.

- In separate bowl, mix whipped topping, dressing, noodles and ½ teaspoon salt.

- Combine dressing mixture with salad and serve immediately. Serves 6 to 8.

TIP: You can make the salad in advance, but mix the dressing right before serving.

TIP: Toasting brings out the flavors of nuts and seeds. Place nuts or seeds on baking sheet and bake at 225° for 10 minutes. Be careful not to burn them.

A "free-range" chicken is one that is given twice as much room as mass produced chickens and they are free to roam indoors and outdoors. This is supposed to enhance the "chicken" flavor because they are "happy" chickens.

Fort Vancouver National Historical Site in Washington was the headquarters for the Hudson's Bay Company's fur trading operations. The historical designation was granted in 1961.

Raisin-Rice Chicken Salad

3 cups instant brown rice
¼ cup (½ stick) butter
3 cups cooked, diced chicken breasts
½ cup golden raisins
½ cup chopped red bell pepper

- Cook brown rice according to package directions. Add butter and a little salt and pepper. While rice is still hot, stir in chicken, raisins and bell pepper. Transfer to serving bowl.

Dressing:

2 tablespoons lemon juice
1 tablespoon dijon-style mustard
2 tablespoons honey
1 teaspoon white wine vinegar
¼ cup slivered almonds, toasted*

- Combine lemon juice, mustard, honey and wine vinegar in jar and shake until ingredients blend well.

- Drizzle over rice-chicken mixture and sprinkle with almonds. Serves 6 to 8.

TIP: Toasting brings out the flavors of nuts and seeds. Place nuts or seeds on baking sheet and bake at 225° for 10 minutes. Be careful not to burn them.

The Columbia River cuts the only route to sea level through the Cascade Mountain Range, 80 miles to the sea. Canyon walls in the Columbia River Gorge reach 4000 feet above water level. The Gorge is part of the border between Oregon and Washington.

Pasta-Turkey Salad Supper

1 (12 ounce) package tri-color spiral pasta
1 (4 ounce) can sliced ripe olives, drained
1 cup broccoli florets
1 cup cauliflower florets
2 small yellow squash, sliced
1 cup halved cherry tomatoes
1 (8 ounce) bottle cheddar-parmesan ranch dressing
1½ pounds hickory-smoked, cracked-pepper turkey breast, cubed

- Cook pasta according to package directions. Drain and rinse in cold water. Combine pasta, olives, broccoli, cauliflower, squash and tomatoes in large salad bowl.

- Toss with dressing. Arranged turkey over salad. Serve immediately. Serves 8 to 10.

Salmon-Caesar Salad

This is a great meal for two. Double it for four.

12 leaves romaine lettuce
Shredded parmesan cheese
Caesar dressing
Croutons
1 (8 ounce) salmon fillet, smoked, cooked or grilled

- Pat romaine leaves dry with paper towels, tear leaves into pieces and place in salad bowl.

- Sprinkle with lots of shredded parmesan and toss with dressing. When ready to serve, sprinkle croutons on top and place strips of salmon on top like spokes of a wheel. Serves 2.

Dungeness Crab-Hazelnut Salad

1½ pounds fresh dungeness crabs
2 tablespoons chopped fresh tarragon
2 tablespoons white wine vinegar
1 tablespoon dijon-style mustard
1 cup hazelnut oil
Sugar
½ cup chopped hazelnuts, roasted
1 bunch watercress, torn
4 large leaves radicchio, torn
3 large leaves romaine, torn

- Cook and clean crabs and set meat in refrigerator. (See cooking and cleaning instructions on page 135.)

- Whisk tarragon, vinegar and mustard in bowl for about 1 minute. Pour oil in very slowly and whisk constantly.

- Add a pinch of salt, pepper and sugar, taste and adjust seasonings. Add hazelnuts and whisk some more. Store in refrigerator.

- When ready to serve, mix watercress, radicchio and romaine in bowl. Whisk dressing to mix and toss gently with greens.

- Divide dressed greens on 6 individual serving plates and sprinkle crabmeat equally on top of each serving. Serve immediately. Serves 6.

Commercial fishing accounts for a growing part of the Pacific Northwest's economy and includes salmon, halibut, bottomfish, rockfish, cod, sablefish and smelt. Oysters, crabs and geoduck clams are abundant in the area.

Sunny Percival Strawberry Soup

1½ cups fresh strawberries
1 cup orange juice
¼ cup honey
½ cup sour cream
½ cup white wine

- Combine all ingredients in blender and puree.

- Chill thoroughly. Stir before serving. Serves 2.

Fresh Avocado Soup

3 ripe avocados
¼ cup fresh lemon juice
1 (10 ounce) can vegetable broth
1 (8 ounce) carton plain yogurt
White pepper
Chopped chives

- Peel avocados, remove seeds and cut into pieces. Immediately put avocados, lemon juice, broth and yogurt into blender and process until smooth.

- Add a little salt and white pepper and refrigerate for several hours. Serve in soup bowls with chopped chives on top. Serves 4.

Cape Flattery on Olympic Peninsula in Washington is the northwestern most point in the 48 contiguous United States.

Spicy Bean Soup

1 (15 ounce) can refried beans
1 (14 ounce) can chicken broth
2 (4 ounce) cans chopped green chilies
2 cloves garlic, minced
2 - 3 jalapeno chilies, seeded, chopped
1 teaspoon chili powder
6 slices bacon
5 ribs celery, chopped
1 bell pepper, seeded, chopped
1 bunch green onions with tops, chopped, divided
1 (8 ounce) package shredded cheddar cheese

- Heat refried beans and chicken broth in large saucepan and whisk beans and broth together. Add green chilies, garlic, jalapenos, ¼ teaspoon black pepper and chili powder and stir well. Reduce heat to low. cook for 10 minutes and stir occasionally.

- Fry bacon in skillet until crisp and drain. In pan drippings saute celery, bell pepper, and about three-fourths of green onions until onions are translucent.

- Crumble bacon and add to bean soup. Add onions, celery, bell pepper and pan drippings and stir well. Bring to a boil, reduce heat to low, cook for 5 minutes and serve immediately.

- Garnish with remaining green onions and cheese. Serves 4.

The highest point in Washington is Mount Rainier in Pierce County, located 54 miles southeast of Seattle, Washington.

Rainy Day Lentil Soup

¼ cup apple juice
1 cup chopped onions
½ cup diced celery
2 (14 ounce) cans chicken broth
1 cup shredded carrots
½ cup shredded sweet potatoes
1 cup dry lentils, sorted, rinsed
1 - 2 tablespoons minced garlic
½ teaspoon cumin

- Bring apple juice to a boil in large saucepan. Add onions and celery and return to boil.

- Add chicken broth, carrots, sweet potatoes, lentils and garlic and bring to a boil.

- Reduce heat to medium, add cumin and cover. Cook for about 30 minutes or until flavors mix. Add a little salt and pepper. Serves 4.

Since antiquity, garlic has been noted for its special powers as a flavor enhancement for foods and for its suspected medicinal uses. Today it may have a positive effect on lowering cholesterol levels, reducing high blood pressure and maybe even fighting off some cancers, but it is not a proven scientific fact as yet.

The Washington border on the north is adjacent to British Columbia, Canada and runs along the 49th parallel except for Vancouver Island. It borders Oregon to the south. This border runs along the 46th parallel and the Columbia River.

Roasted Garlic Soup

4 - 6 cloves garlic
1 tablespoon olive oil, divided
1 onion, finely chopped
2 (14 ounce) cans chicken broth
4 russet potatoes, peeled, diced
2 teaspoons fresh lemon thyme or ½ teaspoon dried thyme
½ cup low-fat yogurt
½ cup shredded gruyere or jarlsberg cheese
Chives or flat-leaf parsley, chopped

- Preheat oven to 375°.

- Remove loose skins and cut pointed end and papery skin from garlic. Rub with 1 teaspoon olive oil. Wrap in foil and place in baking dish.

- Bake for 35 to 40 minutes or until soft; let cool. Squeeze garlic from outer skin into bowl and set aside.

- Heat remaining oil in large saucepan over medium heat and saute onion until tender. Add garlic and saute for 1 minute.

- Add broth, potatoes and thyme. Cover and simmer until potatoes are very tender, about 25 minutes.

- Puree with yogurt in batches in blender. Serve warm in bowls and top with cheese and chopped chives or parsley. Serves 4.

The Pacific Northwest is the only region in the U.S. with the right climate and soil conditions to grow the highly prized pears from Washington and Oregon. The perfect blend of water, volcanic soil, warm days and cool nights are the secrets to the success of the pear orchards that span the river valley regions from north-central Washington to south-central Oregon.

Incredible Broccoli-Cheese Soup

This really is an incredible soup!

1 (10 ounce) package frozen chopped broccoli
3 tablespoons butter
¼ onion, finely chopped
¼ cup flour
1 (16 ounce) carton half-and-half cream
1 (14 ounce) can chicken broth
⅛ teaspoon cayenne pepper
½ teaspoon summer savory
1 (8 ounce) package cubed mild Mexican Velveeta® cheese

- Punch several holes in broccoli package and microwave for 5 minutes. Turn package in microwave and cook for additional 4 minutes. Leave in microwave for 3 minutes.

- Melt butter in large saucepan over low heat and saute onion but do not brown. Add flour, stir and gradually add half-and-half cream, chicken broth, ½ teaspoon salt, ¼ teaspoon pepper, cayenne pepper and savory. Stir constantly and heat until mixture is slightly thick. Do NOT let mixture come to a boil.

- Add cheese, stir and heat until cheese melts. Add cooked broccoli. Serve piping hot. Serves 4 to 6.

Washington's economy is dominated by aviation, software and technology, wheat, apples, beans and other crops, forest products, and fishing. Washington is a major exporter of manufactured goods, foodstuffs, raw materials and hydroelectricity.

Fast Chicken Noodle Soup

1 (3 ounce) package chicken-flavored ramen noodles, broken
1 (10 ounce) package frozen green peas, thawed
1 (4 ounce) jar sliced mushrooms, drained
3 cups cooked, cubed chicken

- Heat 2¼ cups water in large saucepan to boiling. Add ramen noodles, contents of seasoning packet and peas. Heat to boiling, reduce heat to medium and cook for about 5 minutes.

- Stir in mushrooms and chicken and continue cooking over low heat until all ingredients are hot. To serve, spoon into soup bowls. Serves 4 to 6.

15-Minute Turkey Soup

1 (14 ounce) can chicken broth
3 (15 ounce) cans navy beans, rinsed, drained
1 (28 ounce) can diced tomatoes with liquid
2 - 3 cups small chunks white turkey meat
2 teaspoons minced garlic
¼ teaspoon cayenne pepper
Freshly grated parmesan cheese

- Mix all ingredients except cheese in saucepan and heat. Garnish with parmesan cheese before serving. Serves 6.

There are 30 recognized sovereign Indian tribes and seven unrecognized, but culturally distinct, tribes in Washington. Before arrival of European settlers, the area included numerous tribes, especially along the coast, but the diseases brought by the settlers almost wiped out the entire population of Native Americans.

Italian Beefy Veggie Soup

1 pound lean ground beef
2 teaspoons minced garlic
2 (15 ounce) cans Italian stewed tomatoes
2 (14 ounce) cans beef broth
2 teaspoons Italian seasoning
1 (16 ounce) package frozen mixed vegetables
⅓ cup shell macaroni
1 (8 ounce) package shredded Italian cheese

- Cook beef and garlic in large soup pot for 5 minutes. Stir in tomatoes, broth, 1 cup water, seasoning, mixed vegetables, macaroni and a little salt and pepper.

- Bring to a boil, reduce heat and simmer for 10 to 15 minutes or until macaroni is tender.

- Ladle into individual serving bowls and sprinkle several tablespoons cheese over each serving. Serves 8.

Easy Oyster Soup

3 fresh green onions, finely chopped
2 tablespoons butter
1 (12 ounce) container oysters with liquor
1 (1 pint) carton whipping cream
2 cups milk

- Saute green onions in butter in stew pot. Add oysters, cream, milk and a little salt and pepper.

- Cook over low heat until oyster edges begin to curl and mixture is hot, but not boiling. Serves 4.

TIP: *If you want a little snap to this stew, add cayenne pepper to taste.*

Meat and Potato Stew

2 pounds beef stew meat
2 (15 ounce) cans new potatoes, drained
1 (15 ounce) can sliced carrots, drained
2 (10 ounce) cans French onion soup

- Season meat with a little salt and pepper and cook with 2 cups water in large pot for 1 hour. Add potatoes, carrots and onion soup and mix well.

- Bring to a boil, reduce heat and simmer for 30 minutes. Serves 6 to 8.

Land Ho Fish Stew

1 cup chopped celery
½ cup chopped onion
2 tablespoons butter
1 (15 ounce) can whole kernel corn, drained
1 (15 ounce) can stewed tomatoes
2 teaspoons chili powder
¼ cup minced parsley
1 (1 pound) skinless, boneless cod fillet

- Saute celery and onion in butter in large soup pot until translucent. Add 2 cups water.

- Add corn, tomatoes, chili powder and parsley and cook over medium heat until it is steaming hot, about 10 minutes.

- Cut fish into bite-size pieces and add to soup pot. Cook for about 3 minutes or until fish is done. Serve hot. Serves 4.

Crew Stew

If you can open cans, you can make this stew. Don't let the number of ingredients get to you. Leave something out if you get tired of opening cans. If you don't want stew for the crew, cut the recipe in half.

3 pounds beef chuck roast, cubed or ground meat
Canola oil
2 (15 ounce) cans diced tomatoes
2 (32 ounce) cans cocktail vegetable juice
2 (15 ounce) cans green beans, drained
2 (15 ounce) cans field peas with snaps, drained
2 (15 ounce) cans green peas, drained
2 (14 ounce) cans cut okra, drained
2 (16 ounce) packages frozen lima beans
2 (16 ounce) packages frozen yellow corn
1 (16 ounce) package frozen white corn
2 pounds onion, peeled, diced
4 pounds potatoes, peeled, cubed
1 teaspoon dried rosemary

- Brown roast or ground beef in oil in large stew pot. Add remaining ingredients with 1 quart water and a little salt and pepper.

- Simmer all day. Remove excess fat before serving. Serves 16 to 20.

TIP: *This recipe makes enough for several meals so freeze some for later.*

The San Juan Islands Archipelago in Washington has 172 named islands and many unnamed islands in the Salish Sea just north of Puget Sound.

Maritime Oyster Stew

2 (14 ounce) cans chicken broth
1 large onion, chopped
3 ribs celery, sliced
1 red bell pepper, seeded, chopped
2 teaspoons minced garlic
2 (1 pint) cartons fresh oysters, rinsed, drained
½ cup (1 stick) butter
¼ cup flour
2 cups milk
1 tablespoon dried parsley

- Combine broth, onion, celery, bell pepper and garlic in soup pot. Boil, reduce heat and simmer, stirring occasionally, for 30 minutes.

- Boil oysters in 2 cups water in saucepan for 2 minutes and stir often or until edges of oysters begin to curl.

- Remove oysters, coarsely chop half and set aside. Pour oyster stock into soup pot with vegetables.

- Melt butter in saucepan over medium heat, gradually whisk in flour and cook for 1 minute. Add flour mixture to soup pot and simmer, stirring occasionally, for 3 minutes.

- Stir in chopped oysters, milk, parsley and a little salt and pepper. Cook and stir occasionally over medium heat for 8 minutes or until mixture thickens. Stir in remaining whole oysters. Serves 6.

Scuba diving is one of the attractions at the underwater marine reserves of Fort Casey and Deception Pass State Parks in Washington's San Juan Islands.

Sausage-Bean Chowder

2 pounds pork sausage
1 (15 ounce) can pinto beans with liquid
1 (15 ounce) can navy beans with liquid
1 (15 ounce) can kidney beans, drained
2 (15 ounce) cans Mexican stewed tomatoes
2 (14 ounce) cans chicken broth
1 teaspoon minced garlic

- Brown and cook sausage in soup pot and stir until sausage crumbles.

- Add all beans, tomatoes, broth and garlic. Bring to a boil, reduce heat to low and simmer for 20 minutes. Serves 6.

Island Seafood Chowder

3 onions, chopped
2 bell peppers, seeded, chopped
2 ribs celery, sliced
¼ cup olive oil
3 tablespoons flour
3 (15 ounce) cans stewed tomatoes
1 teaspoon minced garlic
1 teaspoon hot sauce
2 pounds medium fresh shrimp, peeled
1 pound fresh lump crabmeat, flaked
1 (12 ounce) carton oysters, drained

- Saute onions, bell peppers and celery in hot oil in soup pot. Add flour and cook for 1 minute, stirring constantly. Stir in tomatoes, garlic, hot sauce and a little salt and pepper. Boil, reduce heat and simmer for 15 minutes.

- Add shrimp, crabmeat and oysters to soup. Cover and simmer for 15 minutes. Serves 8.

San Juan Salmon Chowder

3 tablespoons butter
1 cup chopped carrots
1 cup chopped sweet onion
½ cup chopped celery
1 (14 ounce) can chicken broth
2 large potatoes, peeled, cubed
1½ pounds boneless, skinless salmon fillets
2 cups milk
1 cup half-and-half cream
1 bay leaf
Hot sauce
Oyster crackers

- Melt butter in soup pot and saute carrots, onions and celery until they are translucent. Add chicken broth and potatoes, cover and cook on low heat for about 10 minutes. (Do not cook too fast.)

- Flake salmon into 1 to 1½-inch pieces.

- Pour in milk, half-and-half cream, salmon, bay leaf and a dash of hot sauce.

- Cover and cook over low heat for about 20 minutes. Season with salt and pepper. Serve hot with oyster crackers. Serves 4.

As a general rule, Atlantic salmon are 99% farmed raised and Pacific salmon are 85% wild.

Troubles are easier to take with soup than without.

Old Yiddish Saying

Newport Seafood Chowder

1 small onion, diced
2 tablespoons butter, divided
2 large potatoes, peeled, diced
1½ pounds cooked, chopped crab or fish
1 (10 ounce) can cream of mushroom soup
½ cup milk

- Cook onions with 1 tablespoon butter in large saucepan over low heat until onions are translucent.

- Add potatoes and just enough water to almost cover potatoes. Cover and cook over low heat until potatoes are just tender, about 10 to 15 minutes.

- Add crab, soup, remaining butter and milk. Cover and cook over low heat for about 20 minutes. (Do not boil.) Season with a little salt and white pepper. Serves 4.

To make a good base for soup, use any of the following: canned soups (such as cream of mushroom soup), canned tomatoes, tomato juice, canned chicken broth, homemade stocks, commercial soup bases, clam or seafood broth and the addition of some bacon.

Olympia is the capital of Washington and is considered one of the most beautiful state capital settings in the U.S. Olympia sits on Budd Inlet which connects to Puget Sound and has picturesque views of Mount Rainier and the Olympic Mountain Range.

Vegetables
and
Side Dishes

Washington Facts

World's Largest Building: *Boeing Plant in Everett, Washington*

World's Three Longest Floating Bridges: *Evergreen Point Bridge, Murrow Memorial Bridge, Hood Canal Bridge*

Last Volcanic Eruption: *Mount St. Helens (1980)*

Largest Dam in the U.S.: *Grand Coulee Dam*

Aberdeen Asparagus Bake

4 (10 ounce) cans asparagus
3 eggs, hard-boiled, sliced
⅓ cup milk
1½ cups shredded cheddar cheese
1¼ cups cheese cracker crumbs

- Preheat oven to 350°.

- Place asparagus in 7 x 11-inch baking dish, layer hard-boiled eggs on top and pour milk over casserole.

- Sprinkle cheese on top and add cracker crumbs. Bake for 30 minutes. Serves 8.

Creamy Brussels Sprouts

2 pints fresh brussels sprouts
1 onion, chopped
¼ cup (½ stick) butter
1 (1 pint) carton sour cream

- Take each brussels sprout and cut crisscross mark on bottom of each so tougher ends cook as quickly as tops. Steam or boil sprouts in saucepan until just tender.

- Saute onion in skillet with butter, add sour cream and brussels sprouts and cook over low heat, stirring constantly. Serve immediately. Serves 8.

Many visitors enjoy cycling over the many lanes and roads in Washington's San Juan Islands.

Spokane Baked Cabbage

1 head cabbage
½ red bell pepper, seeded, chopped
1 (10 ounce) can cream of celery soup
1 (8 ounce) package shredded 4-cheese blend

* Preheat oven to 325°.

* Cut cabbage in chunks and layer in sprayed 7 x 11-inch baking dish with bell pepper, soup and cheese.

* Cover and bake for 45 minutes. Serves 8.

Nooksack Creamed Carrots

¼ cup (½ stick) butter
3 tablespoons flour
1½ cups milk
2 (15 ounce) cans sliced carrots

* Melt butter in saucepan and add flour plus ½ teaspoon salt and mix well.

* Add milk, cook over medium heat and stir constantly. Cook until mixture thickens.

* In smaller saucepan, heat carrots and drain. Add carrots to milk mixture and serve hot. Serves 6 to 8.

The most interesting information comes from children, for they tell all they know and then stop.   Mark Twain

Carrots Galore

1 (16 ounce) package baby carrots
¾ cup orange juice
2 tablespoons butter
2 tablespoons brown sugar
½ teaspoon ground cumin

- Combine carrots, orange juice, butter, brown sugar, cumin and ¼ cup water in saucepan.

- Cook on medium-high for about 10 minutes or until carrots are tender and liquid cooks out. Serves 6.

Wenatchee Salsa-Corn

1 cup hot salsa
1 (16 ounce) package frozen whole kernel corn, thawed
¼ teaspoon garlic powder
½ cup shredded Monterey Jack cheese

- Combine hot salsa, corn, garlic powder and ¼ cup water in saucepan. Cook on medium-low heat and stir occasionally for 5 to 7 minutes.

- Pour into serving bowl and sprinkle with cheese. Serves 6.

The Whitman Mission National Historic Site in Washington presents the story of Marcus and Narcissa Whitman, who operated a mission on the Oregon Trail from 1836 to 1847.

Eggplant Frittata

This is a delicious way to serve eggplant for a light lunch and it is rich enough to be served as the main course. You could put it together the day before and cook it just before serving.

3 cups peeled, finely chopped eggplant
½ cup chopped green bell pepper
3 tablespoons extra-light olive oil
1 (8 ounce) jar roasted red peppers, drained, chopped
10 eggs
½ cup half-and-half cream
1 teaspoon Italian seasoning
⅓ cup grated parmesan cheese

- Preheat oven to 325°.

- Cook eggplant and bell pepper in oil in skillet for 2 to 3 minutes, just until tender. Stir in roasted red peppers.

- Combine eggs, half-and-half cream, 1 teaspoon salt, Italian seasoning and ¼ teaspoon pepper in bowl and beat just until they blend well.

- Add eggplant-pepper mixture to egg-cream mixture. Pour into sprayed 10-inch deep-dish pie pan. Cover and bake for about 15 minutes or until center sets.

- Uncover and sprinkle parmesan cheese over top. Return to oven for about 5 minutes, just until cheese melts slightly. Cut into wedges to serve. Serves 6.

Spokane, Washington is the smallest city in history to host a World's Fair. It was originally founded as a fur trading center in 1872.

Green Beans-Mushrooms

½ cup (1 stick) butter, divided
1 small onion, chopped
1 (8 ounce) carton fresh Washington mushrooms, sliced
2 pounds fresh green beans, trimmed
¾ cup chicken broth

- Melt ¼ cup (½ stick) butter in saucepan, saute onion and mushrooms and transfer to small bowl.

- In same saucepan, melt remaining butter and toss with green beans.

- Pour chicken broth over beans and bring to a boil. Reduce heat, cover and simmer until liquid evaporates and green beans are tender-crisp.

- Stir in mushroom mixture and season with a little salt and pepper. Serves 8.

Green Beans with Pine Nuts

1 (16 ounce) package frozen green beans, thawed
¼ cup (½ stick) butter
¾ cup pine nuts
½ teaspoon garlic powder
½ teaspoon celery salt

- Cook beans in ½ cup water in 3-quart saucepan, covered, for 10 to 15 minutes or until beans are tender-crisp and drain.

- Melt butter in skillet over medium heat and add pine nuts. Cook, stirring frequently, until golden.

- Add pine nuts to green beans and season with garlic powder, ½ teaspoon salt, ½ teaspoon pepper and celery salt. Serves 6.

Walla Walla Caramelized Onions

This is very good served with grilled meats.

2 tablespoons butter
4 - 5 Washington Walla Walla sweet onions, thinly sliced
¼ teaspoon garlic powder

- Melt butter in large heavy skillet. Add onion slices, garlic powder and a little salt and pepper and cook slowly on low heat.

- Cook for about 30 minutes, stirring occasionally, until onions are soft and dark golden brown. Serves 6.

Sweet Onion Casserole

This is a great substitute for potatoes or rice.

3 cups cracker crumbs
½ cup (1 stick) butter, melted, divided
4 cups coarsely chopped Washington Walla Walla sweet onions

- Preheat oven to 300°.

- Combine and mix cracker crumbs and ¼ cup (½ stick) butter in bowl. Place mixture in 9 x 13-inch baking dish and pat down. Saute onions in remaining butter and spread over crust.

Sauce:

1 cup milk
2 eggs, slightly beaten
1 teaspoon seasoned salt
1½ cups shredded cheddar cheese

- Combine milk, eggs, seasoned salt, ¼ teaspoon pepper and cheese in saucepan. Cook over low heat until cheese melts.

- Pour over onions on crust and bake for 45 minutes or until knife inserted in center comes out clean. Serves 6.

Roasted Potatoes

18 - 20 small, new (red) potatoes with peels
½ cup (1 stick) butter, melted
2 (4 ounce) cans diced green chilies
2 tablespoons fresh snipped parsley
½ teaspoon garlic powder
½ teaspoon paprika

- Steam potatoes in large saucepan with small amount of water until tender. (Test with fork.)

- In separate saucepan, combine butter, green chilies, parsley, garlic powder, 1 teaspoon salt and ½ teaspoon pepper. Heat until ingredients mix well.

- Place potatoes in serving dish, spoon butter mixture over potatoes and sprinkle with paprika. Serves 6 to 8.

Washington Potatoes

- *Washington supplies 20% of potato production in the U.S. and ranks as the number two producer of potatoes nationwide.*
- *About 90% of all Washington potatoes are processed for french fries, hash browns, potato chips and dehydrated products.*
- *The potato is 80% water and 20% solids.*
- *The average American eats about 126 pounds of potatoes per year compared to 370 pounds of potatoes eaten by Germans.*
- *George Washington introduced french fries to America when he served them at a White House dinner.*

Unbelievable Sweet Potato Casserole

This is the best sweet potato recipe you will ever make!

1 (29 ounce) can sweet potatoes, drained
⅓ cup evaporated milk
¾ cup sugar
2 eggs, beaten
¼ cup (½ stick) butter, melted
1 teaspoon vanilla

- Preheat oven to 350°.

- Place sweet potatoes in bowl and mash slightly with fork.

- Add evaporated milk, sugar, eggs, butter and vanilla and mix well.

- Pour into sprayed 7 x 11-inch baking dish.

Topping:

1 cup packed light brown sugar
⅓ cup butter, melted
½ cup flour
1 cup chopped pecans

- Mix all ingredients in bowl and sprinkle over casserole. Bake for 35 minutes or until crusty on top. Serves 8.

By the end of the Ice Age about 15,000 years ago, the Vashon Glacier had carved out the Puget Sound region. The Grand Coulee in Washington was also created at this time by enormous floods that occured when glacial ice dams broke.

Apricot-Glazed Sweet Potatoes

1½ cups apricot preserves
2 teaspoons lemon juice
½ teaspoon ground nutmeg
¼ teaspoon ground cinnamon
4 sweet potatoes, peeled

- Preheat oven to 400°.

- Cook preserves and ½ cup water in heavy saucepan over medium heat until mixture begins to boil.

- Simmer for 5 minutes and stir constantly. Remove from heat and stir in lemon juice, nutmeg and cinnamon.

- Slice sweet potatoes lengthwise into 8 wedges and baste thoroughly with about half apricot mixture. Bake for 20 minutes.

- Remove from oven and baste with remaining sauce. Bake for additional 20 minutes or until tender. Serves 6 to 8.

I cldnuot blviee that I cluod aulaclty uesdnatnrd waht I was rdgnieg. The phaonmneal pweor of the hmuan mnid. Aoccdrnig to rscheearch at Cmabrigde Uinervtisy, it deosn't mttaer in waht odrer the ltteers in a wrod are, the olny iprmoatnt tnhig is taht the frist and lsat ltteer be in the rghiut pclae.

British explorer George Vancouver and his officers Peter Puget and Joseph Whidbey began charting Puget Sound in 1792.

Evergreen Spinach with Pine Nuts

1 (16 ounce) package frozen leaf spinach, thawed
¼ cup (½ stick) butter
2 cloves garlic, finely minced
5 green onions with tops, chopped
½ teaspoon seasoning salt
¼ teaspoon celery salt
½ cup pine nuts

- Cook spinach according to package directions. Melt butter in saucepan and add garlic, green onions, seasoning salt and celery salt. Mix well, pour over spinach and toss.

- Place in 2-quart baking dish and sprinkle pine nuts over top. Place under broiler, brown nuts slightly and serve hot. Serves 6.

British explorer James Cook named Cape Flattery in what is now Washington in 1778. His reports encouraged European fur trappers and traders to come by sea and land.

The secret of staying young is to live honestly, eat slowly and lie about your age. Lucille Ball

Sunny Yellow Squash

2 pounds small-medium yellow squash, sliced
2 onions, coarsely chopped
3 ribs celery, diagonally sliced
1 red bell pepper, seeded, julienned
1 (8 ounce) package cream cheese, cubed
2 poblano green chilies, seeded, chopped
½ teaspoon sugar
¼ cup (½ stick) butter, melted
1 (10 ounce) can fiesta nacho cheese soup
1½ cups seasoned croutons

- Preheat oven to 350°.

- Combine squash, onions, celery and bell pepper in large saucepan. Add about 1 cup water and cook for about 10 minutes or until tender-crisp. Drain well.

- While still hot, stir in cream cheese, green chilies, sugar, 1 teaspoon salt, 1 teaspoon pepper, butter and soup and stir just enough for cream cheese to melt and blend.

- Pour into sprayed 9 x 13-inch baking dish. Sprinkle croutons on top and bake for about 20 minutes. Serves 8.

TIP: If you don't want black specks in this dish, use white pepper.

The primary pear-growing regions in the Pacific Northwest marketed under the USA Pears logo are 1) on the banks of the Columbia and Hood Rivers below Mt. Adams and Mt. Hood in Washington and Oregon, 2) the Rogue River Valley near Medford, Oregon 3) the Wenatchee Valley in north-central Washington where pear orchards date back to the 1850's and 4) the Yakima Valley in Washington.

Valley Squash Mix

1 large spaghetti squash
1 large bell pepper, seeded, chopped
1 large tomato, seeded, chopped
4 - 5 green onions with tops, chopped
3 ribs celery, chopped
½ cup canola oil
½ cup vinegar

- Boil spaghetti squash in water in saucepan for 45 minutes. Remove from water, cut in half and cool.

- Combine bell pepper, tomato, green onions and celery in large bowl.

- In separate bowl mix oil, vinegar and a little salt and pepper and stir well. Pour over bell pepper mixture and stir.

- Remove seeds from squash and scoop out flesh with fork. Add to vegetables and stir well. Cover and refrigerate for several hours before serving. Serves 6.

Lewis and Clark reached the confluence of the Columbia and Snake Rivers in 1805. They reached the Pacific Ocean the same year.

The British set up Hudson's Bay Company at Fort Vancouver on the banks of the Columbia River in 1825 to establish its western headquarters. Today the site in Washington has been reconstructed to appear much like it was in 1825.

Cascades Stuffed Yellow Squash

5 large yellow squash
1 (16 ounce) package frozen chopped spinach, thawed
1 (8 ounce) package cream cheese, cubed
1 (1 ounce) packet onion soup mix
Shredded cheddar cheese

- Preheat oven to 325°.

- Steam squash whole until tender. Cut squash lengthwise and remove seeds with spoon. Set aside shells.

- Cook spinach according to package directions and drain well. Add cream cheese to spinach and stir until it melts. Do not let this boil. Add soup mix and blend well.

- Fill scooped out squash shells with spinach mixture and top with few sprinkles of cheddar cheese.

- Place on baking sheet and bake for about 15 minutes. Serves 4 to 6.

Middle age is when you've met so many people that every new person you meet reminds you of someone else.
Ogden Nash

In south central Washington the Yakima Indian Tribe has a 1.4 million-acre reservation with a museum and cultural center that preserves the heritage of the Yakimas, also called the Plateau People.

Eureka Baked Tomatoes

2 (15 ounce) cans diced tomatoes, drained
1½ cups toasted breadcrumbs, divided
¼ cup sugar
½ Washington Walla Walla sweet onion, chopped
¼ cup (½ stick) butter, melted

- Preheat oven to 325°.

- Combine tomatoes, 1 cup breadcrumbs, sugar, onion and butter in bowl.

- Pour into sprayed baking dish and cover with remaining breadcrumbs.

- Bake for 25 to 30 minutes or until crumbs are light brown. Serves 6.

Brown Rice and Pine Nuts

1 (6 ounce) box instant brown rice
1 (14 ounce) can beef broth
2 ribs celery, sliced
1 small onion, chopped
¼ cup (½ stick) butter
1 teaspoon grated lemon peel
1 tablespoon chopped fresh cilantro leaves
¼ cup toasted pine nuts

- Cook brown rice according to package directions, using beef broth with water to total amount of liquid in package directions. Let stand for 5 minutes.

- Saute celery and onion in butter in skillet. Fluff rice and add celery, onion, lemon peel, cilantro and pine nuts. Serves 8.

River Gorge Pasta with Basil

2½ cups small tube pasta
1 small onion, chopped
2 tablespoons canola oil
2½ tablespoons dried basil
1 cup shredded mozzarella cheese

- Cook pasta in saucepan according to package directions and drain.

- Saute onion in oil in skillet. Stir in basil, 1 teaspoon salt and ¼ teaspoon pepper. Cook and stir for 1 minute. Add pasta to basil mixture.

- Remove from heat and stir in cheese just until it begins to melt. Serve immediately. Serves 4 to 6.

Bremerton Pasta with Artichokes, Olives and Prosciutto

1 (10 ounce) package rotini or fusilli pasta
1 (10 ounce) jar artichoke hearts with marinade
3 large tomatoes, seeded, chopped, drained
⅓ cup sliced black olives, drained
6 green onions with tops, chopped
½ pound prosciutto, chopped
1 tablespoon mayonnaise

- Prepare pasta according to package directions. Set aside to cool.

- Mix all remaining ingredients with pasta and serve chilled. Serves 4.

Penne with Creamy
Goat Cheese and Walnuts

1 (16 ounce) package penne pasta
1 bunch green onions with tops, chopped
1 cup chopped walnuts
3 - 4 tablespoons canola oil
1 (4 ounce) carton crumbled goat cheese
1 (8 ounce) carton whipping cream
½ cup shredded romano cheese

- Prepare pasta according to package directions and drain.

- Saute green onions and walnuts in hot oil in skillet over medium heat until onions are translucent.

- Add drained pasta and goat cheese to skillet, simmer until goat cheese melts and stir frequently. (Do not scorch cheese.)

- Pour in whipping cream and romano cheese and heat on low. Stir until cheeses are hot. Serve immediately. Serves 4 to 6.

Twelve species of huckleberries grow in Washington and Oregon. They are often grouped as plants producing red or blue berries as well as plants that produce berries in clusters or individually on the twig.

The Columbia River Gorge Scenic Byway is a stretch along the Washington-Oregon border that crosses thick forests and spectacular viewing areas of waterfalls and the Columbia River windsurfers.

Northwest Wild Mushroom Pasta

1 onion, chopped
1 cup chopped celery
1 green bell pepper, seeded, chopped
1 red bell pepper, seeded, chopped
1 (8 ounce) carton fresh mushrooms, sliced
6 tablespoons (¾ stick) butter
1⅓ cups orzo pasta
1 (14 ounce) can beef broth
1 tablespoon Worcestershire sauce
¾ cup chopped walnuts
Chopped green onions with tops

- Preheat oven to 325°.

- Saute onion, celery, bell peppers and mushrooms in butter in skillet.

- Cook orzo in beef broth and 1 cup water in saucepan for 10 to 11 minutes and drain.

- Combine onion-bell pepper mixture, orzo, Worcestershire, walnuts and ½ teaspoon each of salt and pepper in large bowl and mix well.

- Transfer to sprayed 2-quart baking dish. Cover and bake for 30 minutes.

- When ready to serve, sprinkle chopped green onions over top of casserole. Serves 8.

Hurricane Ridge in Olympic National Park in Washington is known for its severe weather, but on sunny days has outstanding views of distant peaks, glaciers and sometimes Vancouver Island.

Main Dishes

Chicken • Beef

Pork • Seafood

Washington Facts

State Folk Song: *"Roll On, Columbia, Roll On"*

State Dance: *Square Dance*

State Song: *"Washington, My Home"*

State Grass: *Bluebunch Wheatgrass*

Columbia Almond-Crusted Chicken

1 egg
¼ cup seasoned breadcrumbs
1 cup sliced almonds
4 boneless, skinless chicken breast halves
1 (5 ounce) package grated parmesan cheese

- Preheat oven to 325°.

- Place egg and 1 teaspoon water in shallow bowl and beat. In separate shallow bowl, combine breadcrumbs and almonds.

- Dip each chicken breast in egg, then in almond mixture and place in sprayed 9 x 13-inch baking pan.

- Bake for 20 minutes. Remove chicken from oven and sprinkle parmesan cheese over each breast. Bake for additional 15 minutes or until almonds and cheese are golden brown. Serve with sauce.

Sauce:

1 teaspoon minced garlic
⅓ cup finely chopped onion
2 tablespoons olive oil
1 cup white wine
¼ cup teriyaki sauce

- Saute garlic and onion in oil in saucepan. Add wine and teriyaki sauce and bring to a boil. Reduce heat and simmer for about 10 minutes or until mixture reduces by half.

- When serving, divide sauce among 4 plates and place chicken breasts on top. Serves 4.

Steelhead trout are found in the Pacific Ocean drainages from southern California to Alaska.

Apricot-Ginger Chicken

2 teaspoons ground ginger
½ cup Italian dressing
4 boneless, skinless chicken breast halves
⅔ cup apricot preserves

- Combine ginger and Italian dressing in bowl and place in large resealable plastic bag. Add chicken to bag, marinate in refrigerator overnight and turn occasionally.

- When ready to bake, preheat oven to 350°.

- Remove chicken and set aside ¼ cup marinade; discard remaining marinade Place chicken in shallow baking dish.

- Pour ¼ cup marinade in saucepan, bring to boil and boil for 1 minute. Remove from heat, stir in apricot preserves and set aside.

- Bake chicken for 45 minutes and brush with marinade mixture last 10 minutes of cooking. Serves 4.

Beware the young doctor and the old barber.
Benjamin Franklin

State Route 542 east of Bellingham climbs to Artist Point where Washington's Mount Shuksan can be seen reflected in the still waters of Picture Lake. The road is generally closed October through June because of snow.

Ephrata Asparagus Chicken

1 (1 ounce) packet hollandaise sauce mix
2 large boneless skinless chicken breasts, cut into strips
Canola oil
1 tablespoon lemon juice
1 (8 ounce) package egg noodles, cooked
1 (15 ounce) can asparagus spears, drained

- Prepare hollandaise sauce according to package directions.

- Cook chicken strips in large skillet with a little oil for 12 to 15 minutes or until brown and stir occasionally.

- Add hollandaise sauce and lemon juice. Cover and cook for additional 10 minutes, stirring occasionally.

- When ready to serve, place chicken over noodles and add hot asparagus spears. Serves 6 to 8.

Leftovers are great for soups. Store in freezer until needed along with meaty bones.

Seafood is a good source of omega-3 fatty acids which are reported to lower risks of cardiac arrest, high cholesterol levels and high blood pressure. In 1995 the Journal of the American Medical Association reported that one serving of fish high in omega-3 fatty acids per week can reduce risk of heart attacks by 50% to 70%.

River Chicken

6 - 8 boneless, skinless chicken breast halves
2 tablespoons canola oil
⅓ cup cornstarch
⅔ cup sugar
½ cup packed brown sugar
1 teaspoon chicken bouillon granules
1 (15 ounce) can pineapple chunks with juice
1½ cups orange juice
½ cup vinegar
¼ cup ketchup
2 tablespoons soy sauce
¼ teaspoon ground ginger
1 red bell pepper, thinly sliced

- Preheat oven to 325°.

- Brown chicken breasts in large skillet with oil. Place in sprayed 10 x 15-inch baking dish.

- Combine cornstarch, sugar, brown sugar and bouillon granules in large saucepan and mix well.

- Drain pineapple and save juice. Add pineapple juice, orange juice, vinegar, ketchup, soy sauce and ginger to cornstarch mixture in saucepan and mix well.

- Cook on high heat, stirring constantly, until mixture thickens. Pour sauce over chicken breasts. Bake for 45 minutes.

- Remove from oven, add pineapple chunks and thinly sliced bell peppers and bake for additional 15 minutes. Serves 6 to 8.

Chicken with Sweet Red Peppers

1 (14 ounce) can chicken broth
1 (8 ounce) can whole kernel corn, drained
2 cups cooked, cubed chicken breasts
1 cup roasted red bell peppers
¼ cup pine nuts, toasted

- Preheat oven to 325°.

- Combine chicken broth, corn, chicken and roasted bell peppers in saucepan over medium-high heat. Cover and simmer for about 10 minutes.

- Spoon into sprayed 7 x 11-inch baking dish, top with pine nuts and bake for 15 minutes. Serves 4.

Rain Forest Chicken and Veggies

1½ pounds chicken breast tenderloins
½ cup (1 stick) butter, divided
1 (6 ounce) box fried rice with seasoning packet
⅛ teaspoon cayenne pepper
¼ cup seeded, chopped red bell pepper
1 (10 ounce) package frozen broccoli spears, thawed
1 (10 ounce) package frozen corn, thawed

- Preheat oven to 350°.

- Brown chicken tenderloins in about 3 tablespoons butter in skillet. Remove chicken to large bowl.

- In same skillet, saute rice with remaining butter until light brown and spoon into bowl with chicken. Add 2½ cups water, cayenne pepper, bell pepper, broccoli spears and corn and mix well.

- Spoon into sprayed 9 x 13-inch baking dish. Cover and bake for 25 minutes or until rice and vegetables are tender. Serves 8.

Orange-Spiced Chicken

⅔ cup flour
½ teaspoon dried basil
¼ teaspoon leaf tarragon
2 - 3 tablespoons canola oil
6 boneless, skinless, chicken breast halves
1 (6 ounce) can frozen orange juice concentrate, thawed
½ cup white wine vinegar
⅔ cup packed brown sugar
1 (6 ounce) box long grain-wild rice, cooked

- Preheat oven to 350°.

- Mix flour, 1 teaspoon salt, ½ teaspoon pepper, basil and tarragon in resealable plastic bag.

- Pour oil into large skillet and heat. Coat chicken in flour mixture and brown both sides of chicken.

- Mix orange juice concentrate, ¼ cup water, vinegar and brown sugar in small bowl.

- When chicken breasts brown, place in sprayed 9 x 13-inch baking dish, cover with orange juice mixture and bake for 1 hour. Serve chicken and orange sauce over rice. Serves 6.

Pike Place Market in Seattle, Washington is well known for its fishmongers who throw the catch of the day for spectators. It is a farmers market filled with vendors of all kinds.

Prairie Spring Chicken

2 pounds chicken thighs
Canola oil
¾ cup chili sauce
¾ cup packed brown sugar
1 (1 ounce) packet onion soup mix
⅛ teaspoon cayenne pepper
Rice, cooked

- Preheat oven to 325º.

- Brown chicken pieces in skillet with a little oil and place in sprayed 9 x 13-inch baking dish.

- Combine chili sauce, brown sugar, soup mix, cayenne pepper and ½ cup water in bowl and pour over chicken.

- Cover and bake for 20 minutes. Remove cover and bake for additional 15 minute to brown. Serve over rice. Serves 8.

Sweet-and-Sour Cranberry Chicken

1 (10 ounce) jar sweet-and-sour sauce
1 (1 ounce) packet onion soup mix
1 (16 ounce) can whole cranberry sauce
6 boneless, skinless chicken breast halves

- Preheat oven to 325°.

- Combine sweet-and-sour sauce, onion soup mix and cranberry sauce in bowl.

- Place chicken breasts in sprayed 9 x 13-inch shallow baking dish. Pour cranberry mixture over chicken breasts.

- Cover and bake for 30 minutes. Uncover and bake for additional 25 minutes or until juices run clear. Serves 6.

Stir-Fry Chicken

Canola oil
1 pound chicken tenders, cut into strips
1 (16 ounce) package frozen broccoli, cauliflower and carrots
1 (8 ounce) jar stir-fry sauce
1 (12 ounce) package chow mein noodles

- Heat a little oil and stir-fry chicken strips in 12-inch wok or skillet over high heat for about 4 minutes.

- Add vegetables and stir-fry for additional 4 minutes or until vegetables are tender. Stir in stir-fry sauce and cook just until mixture is hot. Serve over chow mein noodles. Serves 8 to 10.

Pacific Turkey Burgers

2 pounds ground turkey
1 (16 ounce) jar hot chipotle salsa, divided
8 slices Monterey Jack cheese
Sesame seed hamburger buns

- Preheat broiler.
- Combine ground turkey with 1 cup salsa in large bowl. Mix well and shape into 8 patties.
- Place patties on broiler pan and broil for 12 to 15 minutes. Turn once during cooking. Top each patty with cheese slice and heat just long enough to melt cheese.
- Place burgers on buns, spoon heaping tablespoon salsa over cheese and top with remaining half of bun. Serves 6 to 8.

The longest recorded flight by a domestic chicken is 13 seconds. They can travel up to 9 miles per hour..

Turkey Tenders with Honey-Ginger Glaze

Canola oil
1 pound turkey tenders
Rice, cooked

- Place a little oil in heavy skillet and cook turkey tenders for about 5 minutes on each side or until they brown.

Glaze:

⅔ cup honey
2 teaspoons peeled grated fresh ginger
1 tablespoon marinade for chicken
1 tablespoon soy sauce
1 tablespoon lemon juice

- Combine all glaze ingredients, mix well and pour into skillet with turkey. Bring mixture to a boil, reduce heat and simmer for 15 minutes. Serve over rice. Serves 6.

TIP: As a time-saver, you might want to try the package of rice that can be microwaved for 90 seconds and it's ready to serve.

Steptoe Butte is a thimble-shaped natural monument of quartzite which rises 3,612 feet above southeast Washington's flat lands.

Ginger Orange-Glazed Cornish Hens

1 cup fresh orange juice
2 tablespoons plus ½ teaspoon peeled, minced fresh ginger,
  divided
1 tablespoon soy sauce
3 tablespoons honey
2 (1½ pounds) cornish hens, halved

- Preheat oven to 400°.

- Combine orange juice, 2 tablespoons minced ginger, soy
  sauce and honey in saucepan and cook on high heat, stirring
  constantly, for 3 minutes or until thick and glossy.

- Place hens in sprayed 9 x 13-inch baking pan and sprinkle
  ½ teaspoon ginger and ½ teaspoon each of salt and pepper
  over birds.

- Spoon glaze mixture over hens and bake for 25 minutes. Brush
  glaze over hens several times while cooking. Serves 2.

Before squeezing the juice from lemons, limes or oranges, scrape the outside rind to get just the colored part of the rind (called zest). Even if your recipe doesn't call for it, save it in air-tight plastic bags for flavoring all kinds of dishes.

Seasoned Beef Tenderloin

3 tablespoons dijon-style mustard
2 tablespoons prepared horseradish
1 (3 pound) center-cut beef tenderloin
½ cup seasoned breadcrumbs

- Combine mustard and horseradish in bowl and spread over beef tenderloin.

- Press breadcrumbs into horseradish-mustard mixture and wrap in foil. Refrigerate for at least 12 hours.

- When ready to bake, preheat oven to 375°.

- Remove wrap and place on sprayed pan. Bake for 30 minutes or to 145° for medium rare. Let tenderloin stand for 15 minutes before slicing. Serves 6.

Skillet Sirloin

2 teaspoons canola oil
2 teaspoons minced garlic
½ teaspoon cayenne pepper
2 tablespoons soy sauce
2 tablespoons honey
1 pound beef sirloin, thinly sliced
Rice, cooked

- Combine oil, garlic, cayenne pepper, soy sauce and honey in bowl and place in resealable plastic bag.

- Add sliced beef, seal bag and shake. Refrigerate for 30 minutes.

- Place beef mixture in large, sprayed skillet over medium-high heat. Cook for 5 to 6 minutes or until desired doneness, but do not overcook. Serve over rice. Serves 4 to 5.

Oriental Beef, Noodles and Veggies

2 (4.4 ounce) packages Thai sesame noodles
1 pound sirloin steak, cut in strips
Canola oil
1 (16 ounce) package frozen stir-fry vegetables, thawed
½ cup chopped peanuts

- Cook noodles according to package directions. Remove from heat and cover. Season sirloin strips with salt and pepper.

- Add half sirloin strips to skillet with a little oil, brown and cook for 2 minutes and remove to bowl. Cook remaining steak and remove to bowl.

- In same skillet, place vegetables and ½ cup water, cover and cook for 5 minutes or until tender-crisp.

- Remove from heat, add steak strips and toss to mix. Serve over noodles and sprinkle with chopped peanuts. Serves 6 to 8.

Washington's wine country is located in Yakima County and is in the same latitude as the world famous wine country in France.

Washington is a leading producer of lumber. Trees in the area include Douglas fir, hemlock, ponderosa pine, white pine, spruce and cedar.

Tumwater Spicy Pepper Steak

1½ - 2 pounds sirloin or round steak
2 tablespoons canola oil
1 teaspoon garlic powder
¾ teaspoon ground ginger
1 teaspoon seasoned salt
3 green bell peppers, chopped
1 onion, chopped
1 cup sliced celery
2 tablespoons cornstarch
¼ cup soy sauce
1 teaspoon sugar
1 (14 ounce) can beef broth
1 (4 ounce) can sliced mushrooms, drained
1 (10 ounce) can tomatoes and green chilies, drained
Rice or noodles, cooked

- Cut steak into very thin strips. (It will slice easier if frozen for 1 hour.)

- Heat oil in large skillet or roasting pan, brown steak and add garlic powder, ginger, seasoned salt and ½ teaspoon pepper. Remove meat and saute green peppers, onion and celery for 3 minutes.

- Dissolve cornstarch in a little cold water in bowl. Add steak to skillet or roasting pan and add soy sauce, sugar, beef broth, cornstarch, mushrooms, and tomatoes and green chilies.

- Bring ingredients to a boil then simmer for 30 minutes. (If you prefer, place in 3-quart baking dish and bake at 350° for 40 minutes.) Serve over rice or noodles. Serves 10 to 12.

Grilled Steak with Garlic-Mustard Sauce

⅓ cup apple juice
2 tablespoons dijon-style mustard
1 tablespoon minced garlic
4 (1 inch) thick boneless beef top strip steaks

- Combine apple juice, mustard, garlic and 1 teaspoon pepper in bowl and mix well. Set aside ¼ cup sauce for basting. Brush steaks with remaining sauce.

- Cook steaks on grill over medium hot coals (or under broiler or in skillet). Grill for about 10 to 15 minutes or until desired doneness and turn occasionally.

- During last 8 to 10 minutes of grilling, baste steaks with the ¼ cup sauce set aside for basting. Serves 4.

If stored properly, unopened fresh garlic bulbs stay fresh for six to eight weeks before beginnings to dry out and lose some flavor. The best way to store garlic bulbs is in an open container in a dark, cool place. Once cloves are separated from the bulb, they will last only one week or so before they begin to dry out.

The Rosellini (Evergreen Point) Bridge in Washington is the largest floating bridge in the world and crosses Lake Washington, connecting Seattle to the cities on the east side of the lake.

Plateau Tomato-Cilantro Steak

1 - 1½ pounds well trimmed round steak, tenderized
Flour
Canola oil
2 onions, chopped
5 carrots, sliced
¾ teaspoon garlic powder
1 (15 ounce) can diced tomatoes with liquid
¾ cup salsa
2 teaspoons beef bouillon granules
¼ cup snipped cilantro

- Preheat oven to 325°.

- Cut meat into serving-size pieces and sprinkle with a little salt and pepper. Dredge steak pieces in flour and coat well. Heat oil in large skillet and brown meat on both sides.

- Remove steak to 9 x 13-inch baking dish. Add onions and carrots and cover.

- In same skillet, combine garlic powder, tomatoes, salsa, ½ cup water, beef bouillon, cilantro and 1 teaspoon salt.

- Heat and stir just to boiling point and pour over steak, onions and carrots. Cover and bake for about 1 hour 10 minutes. Serves 6 to 8.

Spanish explorers first circumnavigated Washington's San Juan Islands in 1791.

Trappers Pepper Steak

This is an easy way to fix steak!

¼ cup plus 1 tablespoon flour, divided
1½ pounds round steak, cut in ½-inch strips
¼ cup canola oil
1 (15 ounce) can diced tomatoes, drained
½ cup chopped onion
1 small clove garlic, minced
1 tablespoon beef bouillon granules
1½ teaspoons Worcestershire sauce
2 large green peppers, seeded, cut in strips
Rice, cooked

- Combine ¼ cup flour, ½ teaspoon salt and ¼ teaspoon pepper in bowl and coat steak. Heat oil in large skillet and brown meat on both sides.

- Add tomatoes, 1 cup water, onion, garlic and bouillon. Cover and simmer for 1 hour 15 minutes or until meat is tender.

- Uncover and add Worcestershire sauce and green pepper strips. Cover again and simmer for additional 5 minutes. Thicken gravy with mixture of 1 tablespoon flour and cold water. Serve over rice. Serves 4 to 6.

Spain ceded its original Pacific Northwest claims to the U.S. in the Transcontinental Treaty of 1819.

Mountain Range Marinated Tri-Tip Roast

2 cloves garlic, minced
⅔ cup soy sauce
¼ cup canola or virgin olive oil
¼ cup packed light brown sugar
2 tablespoons red wine vinegar
1 teaspoon ground ginger
1 (2 - 3 pound) tri-tip roast

- Mix garlic, soy sauce, oil, brown sugar, vinegar and ginger in bowl. Pour into resealable plastic bag with tri-tip.

- Marinate in refrigerator overnight. Turn plastic bag several times to rotate meat.

- Cook slowly over charcoal fire until meat is tender. Cut thin slices across grain. Serves 6.

Savory Rib Roast

1 tablespoon dried thyme
1 tablespoon dried crushed rosemary
1 teaspoon rubbed sage
1 (4 - 5 pound) rib roast

- Preheat oven to 350°.

- Combine thyme, rosemary and sage in small bowl and rub over roast.

- Place roast fat-side up on rack in large roasting pan. Bake for 2 hours to 2 hours 30 minutes or until meat reaches desired doneness.

- Remove roast to warm serving platter and let stand for 10 minutes before slicing. Serves 6 to 8.

Aloha Ocean Pork

This is great served over rice.

2 (1 pound) lean pork tenderloins
1 tablespoon canola oil
1 (15 ounce) can pineapple chunks with juice
1 (12 ounce) bottle chili sauce
1 teaspoon ground ginger
Rice, cooked

- Cut pork in 1-inch bite-sized pieces. Season pork with salt and pepper and brown on medium-high heat in skillet with oil.

- Add pineapple with juice, chili sauce and ginger.

- Cover and simmer for 30 minutes. Serve over rice. Serves 4 to 6.

Pork Tenderloin with Zucchini

2 pounds pork tenderloin, cubed
1 small onion, diced
1 green bell pepper, seeded, diced
2 cloves garlic, minced
1 teaspoon ground cumin
3 tomatoes, diced
1½ pounds squash or zucchini, cubed
1 (15 ounce) can whole kernel corn

- Brown pork in skillet over medium heat and add onion and bell pepper. Cover and cook on low for 15 minutes.

- Add garlic, cumin and tomatoes and cook for additional 10 minutes.

- Add squash, cover and cook for 30 minutes. Add corn and 1 teaspoon salt and simmer for 30 minutes. Serves 6 to 8.

Pork Loin with Apricot Glaze

1 (3½ - 4 pound) center-cut pork loin
1 tablespoon olive oil
Seasoned pepper
1 teaspoon dried rosemary
1 cup dry white wine or cooking wine
1½ cups apricot preserves

- Preheat oven to 350°.

- Rub pork loin with olive oil and sprinkle seasoned pepper and rosemary over roast. Place loin in shallow roasting pan. Pour wine and 1 cup water into pan, cover and roast for 1 hour.

- Remove pan from oven and spoon about 1 cup pan drippings into small bowl. Add apricot preserves and mix well. Pour mixture over pork, reduce oven to 325°, cover and return to oven. Continue to roast for additional 1 hour and baste 2 to 3 times with pan drippings.

- Set aside pork for 15 minutes before slicing. Remove roast from drippings, place in glass baking dish and slice.

- Serve immediately or pour drippings into separate container and refrigerate both. When ready to serve, heat drippings and pour over roast. Warm roast at 350° for 20 minutes. Serves 8.

John Jacob Astor's Pacific Fur Company established Fort Okanogan in 1811 and Fort Spokane in Washington in 1812.

Prizing-Winning Pork Tenderloin

⅔ cup soy sauce
⅔ cup olive oil
2 tablespoons crystallized ginger, finely chopped
2 tablespoons real lime juice
1 teaspoon garlic powder
2 tablespoons minced onion
2 (1 - 2 pound) pork tenderloins

- Combine soy sauce, olive oil, ginger, lime juice, garlic powder and minced onion in bowl and pour over pork tenderloins. Marinate for about 36 hours.

- Cook over charcoal fire for about 45 minutes. Serves 8 to 10.

Apple Valley Pork Chops

These pork chops just melt in your mouth!

6 thick-cut pork chops
Flour
Canola oil
3 baking apples

- Preheat oven to 325°.

- Dip pork chops in flour and coat well.

- Brown pork chops in oil in skillet and place in sprayed 9 x 13-inch baking dish. Add ⅓ cup water to casserole. Cover and bake for 45 minutes.

- Peel, halve and seed apples and place half apple over each pork chop. Return to oven for 5 to 10 minutes. (DO NOT overcook apples). Serves 6.

Parmesan-Covered Pork Chops

½ cup grated parmesan cheese
⅔ cup Italian seasoned dried breadcrumbs
1 egg
4 - 5 thin-cut pork chops
Canola oil

- Combine cheese and dried breadcrumbs in shallow bowl. Beat egg with 1 teaspoon water on shallow plate.

- Dip each pork chop in beaten egg then in breadcrumb mixture.

- Cook with a little oil in skillet over medium-high heat for about 5 minutes on each side or until golden brown. Serves 4 to 5.

Tangy Pork Chops

4 - 6 pork chops
¼ cup Worcestershire sauce
¼ cup ketchup
½ cup honey

- Preheat oven to 325°.

- Brown pork chops in skillet. Place in shallow baking dish. Combine Worcestershire, ketchup and honey in bowl. Pour over pork chops.

- Cover and bake for 20 minutes; uncover and bake for additional 15 minutes. Serves 4 to 6.

Dry onion soup mix sprinkled over a roast that will be sealed in foil makes a delicious gravy while the roast is cooking.

Apple-Glazed Pork Roast

1 (12 ounce) jar apple jelly
4 teaspoons dijon-style mustard
3 teaspoons lemon juice, divided
¼ teaspoon garlic powder
1 (3 - 4 pound) pork loin roast
3 tablespoons brandy

- Preheat oven to 350°.

- Melt jelly in small saucepan over low heat. Stir in mustard and 1 teaspoon lemon juice and set aside. Rub roast with a little black pepper and garlic powder.

- Place on rack in foil-lined shallow roasting pan and bake for about 45 minutes. Remove from oven, brush with jelly mixture and bake for 20 minutes.

- Brush once more with jelly mixture, reduce heat to 325° and bake for additional 1 hour. Remove roast to warm platter.

- Scrape any browned drippings into remaining jelly mixture. Add 2 teaspoons lemon juice and brandy to mixture, bring to a boil and turn heat off.

- To serve, sauce plate and place thin slices of roast on top or serve roast on platter with sauce. Serves 6 to 8.

Washington produces more apples, raspberries, lentils, hops, pears, sweet cherries and spearmint oil than any other state in the U.S. Additional major agricultural crops include apricots, asparagus, grapes, peppermint oil and potatoes.

Citrus-Glazed Ham

Whole cloves
7 - 9 pound butt-end ham, partially cooked
1 (15 ounce) can chunk pineapple with juice
Maraschino cherries, optional

- Preheat oven to 350°.

- Insert lots of whole cloves on outside of ham. Use toothpicks to place pineapple chunks on ham. Set aside pineapple juice. Add cherry on top of pineapple chunk, if you like.

Sauce:

1 cup red wine or cooking wine
1 cup packed brown sugar
Scant tablespoon cut-up crystallized ginger
1½ teaspoons dijon-style mustard
1 (8 ounce) crushed pineapple

- Combine wine, brown sugar, crystallized ginger, mustard, crushed pineapple and juice from chunk pineapple in saucepan and bring to a boil. Turn off heat.

- Place ham in roasting pan and pour hot sauce over ham. Bake for 10 to 15 minutes per pound and baste with sauce every 20 minutes. Serves 10 to 12.

Most of the salmon in North America comes from Pacific waters with about 90% coming from Alaskan waters. King Salmon and Chinook are the most expensive and considered the top of the line. The coho or silver salmon has a firm texture and red-orange color. The sockeye or red salmon has a very red meat and is used primarily for canning.

Seafood Batters

Batters create a crunchy crust on the outside and moist inside when pan-fried or deep-fried. Batters with flour or cornmeal bases usually take 20 or 30 minutes for gluten to activate. Seafood is coated with batter and dropped into hot oil at about 180° to 190° until outside is brown.

Tempura batters and light fish and chips crusts are made at the last minute and fried with no time allowed for gluten to activate. Fish and chips are usually fried in oil that is 370° for 5 seconds or so.

Here are several different batters good for pan-fried or deep-fried seafood. Amounts will all vary with the amount of seafood being cooked.

Simple Basic Batter

- Sprinkle a little salt and pepper in flour and dredge seafood in it to coat. Shake off excess flour and fry. You can substitute breadcrumbs or seasoned breadcrumbs for the flour.
- Carefully place in hot oil, cook and drain on paper towels.

Beer Batter

1 cup flour
8 ounces beer

- Sprinkle a little salt and pepper in flour in bowl and mix with beer. Add a little more flour or beer to get the consistency you like.
- Dip seafood in batter and pan-fry or deep-fry in hot oil. Drain on paper towels.

Washington is second only to California in wine production in the U.S.

3-Step Seafood Batter

Flour
1 egg, beaten
Breadcrumbs or seasoned breadcrumbs

- Sprinkle a little salt and pepper in flour in bowl. Dip seafood in beaten egg and then in flour. Roll seafood in breadcrumbs and fry in hot oil. Drain on paper towels.

Spicy Seafood Batter

1 cup flour
1 cup cornmeal
1 tablespoon garlic salt
2 cups milk
1 tablespoon cayenne pepper
1 tablespoon hot sauce

- Mix flour and cornmeal with a little garlic salt and pepper in bowl. In separate bowl, mix milk, cayenne pepper and hot sauce.

- Dip seafood into flour and shake once to remove excess flour. Transfer seafood to milk mixture and cover all sides. Dredge seafood through flour again, dust off excess and fry in hot oil.

Tempura Batter

⅔ cup flour
⅓ cup cornmeal
1 tablespoon baking powder
1 egg, beaten
1 cup ice water

- Mix flour, cornmeal, baking powder and a little salt and pepper in bowl. In separate bowl, add ice water to egg and whip to mix. Dredge seafood in ice water mixture and coat with flour-cornmeal mixture. Fry in hot oil.

Percival Fish Tacos with Pesto

¾ pound boned white fish
2 tablespoons lime juice
Canola oil
6 - 8 corn tortillas
Shredded lettuce
Finely chopped tomatoes

- Season fish with lime juice and pepper. Cook fish in skillet with a little oil for about 2 minutes on each side until fish flakes easily. Shred each piece of fish and set aside.

- Wrap about 5 tortillas in slightly damp paper towel and heat tortillas in microwave for 45 seconds.

- Place about 2 tablespoons shredded fish, lettuce and tomatoes in tortilla and fold over. Serve immediately with pesto.

Pesto:

1 cup packed cilantro leaves
2 teaspoons lime juice
1 teaspoon minced garlic
¼ cup parmesan cheese
⅓ cup olive oil

- Mix all ingredients in bowl and serve with Percival Fish Tacos. Serves 6.

Steelhead trout and rainbow trout are river spawners and usually appear in the same rivers as Chinook salmon, especially the Columbia, Snake and Skeena Rivers as well as other large rivers in the Pacific Northwest.

Grilled Tuna with Roasted Chile Salsa

4 - 5 poblano chilies
2 mild jalapeno peppers
1 red bell pepper
1 yellow bell pepper
1 large Walla Walla sweet onion, minced
4 - 5 cloves garlic, minced
¼ cup extra-virgin olive oil
¼ cup fresh lime juice
¼ cup snipped cilantro or oregano
4 - 6 tuna steaks

- Roast poblano chilies, by holding chilies over open-flame gas burner with long metal fork or broil in oven until outside turns dark brown on all sides. (Be careful not to burn holes through skin.)

- Place chilies in resealable plastic bag, seal and allow to sweat for about 15 to 20 minutes so skin will slide off easily. Remove skins and cut through length of chile on one side. Remove seeds, but leave veins intact.

- Remove seeds and veins from jalapenos and bell peppers. Chop or mince peppers and mix with all remaining ingredients except fish in bowl. Add a little salt and pepper.

- Cook tuna steaks on each side for about 3 minutes over hot coals or until grill marks show. Check center of steaks and remove from grill just when pink in center is almost gone. Do not overcook and dry out fish.

- Serve hot with salsa on top. Serves 4 to 6.

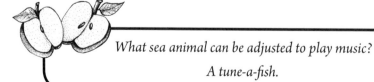

What sea animal can be adjusted to play music?
A tune-a-fish.

Grilled Halibut with Cilantro-Citrus Sauce

3 large pink grapefruit, divided
3 cloves garlic, minced
2 teaspoons chili powder
2 teaspoons ground cumin
½ cup canola oil
¼ cup white wine
4 - 5 (1 inch) halibut steaks
2 teaspoons butter
1 tablespoon cornstarch
¼ cup snipped cilantro

- Cut 1 grapefruit in half and squeeze to measure 1 cup juice in 4-cup measuring cup. Peel remaining grapefruit, divide into sections and refrigerate until ready to use.

- Add garlic, chili powder, cumin, 1 teaspoon salt, oil and white wine to grapefruit juice and mix.

- Place halibut steaks in flat, glass dish and pour ¾ cup marinade over steaks. Cover dish and refrigerate for about 1 hour.

- Prepare charcoal or wood fire and grill. Before grilling, pour about ½ cup marinade from halibut dish into small saucepan and add butter. Pour remaining marinade into measuring cup.

- Add cornstarch to marinade in measuring cup and stir until it dissolves. Pour liquid with cornstarch into saucepan and bring to a boil. Reduce heat and cook until sauce thickens slightly.

- Add cilantro and simmer while steaks cook. Place steaks on grill for about 3 to 5 minutes and turn to cook other side. Cook for about 3 minutes or just until fish is not quite translucent in center.

- To serve, place each halibut steak on plate and pour several tablespoons cilantro sauce over top of each. Garnish with grapefruit sections and serve immediately. Serves 4 to 5.

Lemon-Dill Cod

½ cup mayonnaise
2 tablespoons lemon juice
½ teaspoon grated lemon peel
1 teaspoon dill weed
1 pound cod fillets

- Combine mayonnaise, lemon juice, lemon peel and dill weed in bowl until they blend well.

- Place fish on sprayed grill or broiler rack. Brush with half sauce. Grill or broil for 5 to 8 minutes, turn and brush with remaining sauce.

- Continue grilling or broiling for 5 to 8 minutes or until fish flakes easily with fork. Serves 4.

Spicy Grilled Halibut Steaks

4 (1 inch) thick fresh halibut steaks
1 teaspoon cumin
½ teaspoon cayenne
2 tablespoons spicy brown mustard
1 tablespoon butter, melted
1 lemon

- Rinse halibut steaks and pat dry with paper towels. Sprinkle with cumin, cayenne, spicy mustard and a little salt and pepper.

- Place on grill over medium heat or place under broiler and cook for about 3 minutes per side. (Do not overcook.)

- Remove fish, pour hot butter over top with a squeeze of lemon and serve with slices of lemon. Serves 4.

Snohomish River Deep-Fried Steelhead

Steelhead trout are also known as freshwater salmon.

Steelhead fillets
Milk
Garlic salt
Eggs, beaten
Flour
Instant potato flakes
Canola oil

- Soak fillets in milk overnight. Season with a little garlic salt and pepper. Dip fillets into eggs and dredge through flour.

- Roll fillets in potato flakes and carefully drop into hot oil in deep fryer. Fry until golden brown. Drain and serve hot.

Grilled Steelhead Special

1 whole cleaned steelhead
Onion, minced
Celery, diced
Parsley, snipped
Fresh garlic cloves, minced
Butter
Bacon

- Use these basic ingredients with any size steelhead. Fill cavity of fish with onion, celery, parsley, garlic and butter and season with a little salt and pepper.

- Wrap entire fish with bacon slices. Wrap several times in heavy-duty foil to prevent any leakage. Cook over hot charcoal fire for about 20 minutes on each side. The larger the fish, the longer it will need to cook. Serves 2.

River-Run Baked Rainbow Trout

1 pound trout fillets
3 tablespoons plus ¼ cup butter, divided
1 teaspoon tarragon
2 teaspoons capers
2 tablespoons lemon juice

- Preheat oven to 375°.

- Place fish fillets with 3 tablespoons butter in sprayed shallow pan and sprinkle with salt and pepper.

- Bake for about 6 to 8 minutes, turn and bake until fish flakes. (Do not overcook.)

- For sauce, melt ¼ cup butter with tarragon, capers and lemon juice in saucepan and serve over warm fish. Serves 4 to 6.

Salmon Cakes

2 (15 ounce) cans salmon with liquid, flaked
1 large onion, minced
2 slices white bread, crumbled
2 eggs, beaten
1 tablespoon flour
1 cup canola oil

- Mix all ingredients, except oil, and a little salt and pepper in bowl and shape into 4 patties.

- Heat small amount of oil in large skillet and cook patties over medium heat until brown on both sides. Add oil as needed. Serves 6 to 8.

Issaquah Pistachio-Buttered Salmon

½ cup (1 stick) butter
8 - 10 leaves fresh basil, minced
1 clove garlic, minced
Lime juice
¼ cup shelled pistachios
4 (6 ounce/1½ inches) thick, skinless salmon fillets
½ cup white wine

- Preheat oven to 350°.

- Blend butter, basil, garlic, a little lime juice and pistachios in food processor until smooth and set aside or refrigerate until ready to use.

- Rinse and dry salmon fillets, place them in sprayed glass baking dish. Pour white wine over fillets and season with a little salt and pepper.

- Bake until slightly opaque, about 4 minutes. (Do not overcook.) Remove from oven and spread butter mixture over top. Continue baking until fillets are still slightly pink inside. Serves 4.

More than 200,000 people attend the annual Issaquah Salmon Days Festival in early October. The festival coincides with the arrival of Pacific salmon in Issaquah Creek in Washington, the destination point of their 40-mile trip from Puget Sound.

Easy Breezy Salmon on a Plank

If you haven't tried cooking on a western red cedar plank, you're missing a treat. Here's a super sweet (meaning easy) way to cook fish with lots of flavor.

¾ cup (1½ sticks) butter, softened
⅓ cup snipped fresh basil
4 - 5 cloves garlic, minced or crushed
1 (2 pound) skinless salmon fillet

- Soak cedar plank for about 30 minutes, turn plank over and soak for additional 30 minutes.

- Prepare charcoal grill while cedar plank is soaking. Mix butter, basil and garlic in small bowl and spread it on both sides of salmon.

- When coals are hot, but not flaming, place salmon on plank and plank on grill. Close lid and cook about 5 minutes.

- Check plank to make sure it's not burning and fire to make sure it's not too hot. (Use spray bottle with water to douse plank if it catches on fire.) Add a little salt and pepper on both sides and turn salmon to cook other side.

- Check again after 5 minutes or so and cook until salmon flakes, but is still moist inside. Cooking time varies with fire.

Even with the high content of fats in the Chinook salmon, all salmon are rated highly for their protein, B-group vitamins, vitamin A and omega-3 oils.

Dungeness Crab

One of the real delicacies of the Pacific Northwest is Dungeness crab. Cook it whole or cook legs and claws. It just doesn't get much better than this seafood treasure. You will find instructions for cooking and cleaning crab on the next page. Here are some sauces you may want to try to go with it or just go with the simplest way to eat it… with melted butter or mayonnaise.

Lemon-Garlic Butter

½ cup (1 stick) butter
½ cup extra virgin olive oil
4 cloves garlic, minced
Seasoned salt
Hot sauce
1 lemon, halved

- Melt butter in saucepan and remove from heat. Add olive oil, minced garlic, a pinch of seasoned salt and several drops of hot sauce.
- Squeeze 1 tablespoon fresh lemon juice into mixture and taste. Adjust seasonings and add more lemon juice if needed.

Creamy Basil Dipping Sauce

⅓ cup mayonnaise
⅓ cup sour cream
¼ cup packed, minced fresh basil
2 cloves garlic, minced
1 lemon, halved

- Mix all ingredients except lemon. Season with a little salt and pepper and add fresh lemon juice to taste.

Creamy Lemon-Garlic Sauce

½ cup mayonnaise
2 cloves garlic, minced
2 - 3 green onions with green stems, minced
1 lemon, halved

- Mix all ingredients except lemon. Season with a little salt and pepper and add fresh lemon juice to taste.

How to Cook Dungeness Crab

Step 1:   Rinse fresh crab and place in freezer for about 45 minutes before cooking. Freezing them slows them down just enough so they are easier to handle. (Some people think it's a more humane way to cook live crab because freezing puts them in a dormant state. Skip this step if you don't care about the feelings of the little crab you are about to eat.)

Step 2:   Fill large stock pot with enough water to more than cover crab.

Step 3:   Add about ¼ cup salt for each gallon of water.

Step 4:   Boil water and drop crab into pot. Cover and cook for about 10 to 20 minutes.

Step 5:   Remove crab from water with long tongs and put in ice water. This will stop the cooking and make them cooler to handle for cleaning.

How to Clean Cooked Crab

Step 1:   Hold crab, belly-side down, with one hand and pull the shell away from the body with the other hand.

Step 2:   Flip the crab over and remove the triangular-shaped section of shell.

Step 3:   Flip crab again and remove the gills on both sides with a spoon. Also, remove the intestines running down the center of the back. Also, remove the yellow, mushy stuff that some people treasure and call "crab butter". (Keep it if you have a special use for it.)

(continued next page)

(continued from previous page)

Step 4: Twist off legs and put to one side.

Step 5: Wash body and break in half.

Step 6: Crack legs with mallet or crab cracker and dig or pick out the meat. Remove meat the best way you can. It may not be pretty, but you want every morsel. After all, this is a lot of trouble, but the rewards are worth it.

How to Shuck Clams

Clams should be alive before they are cooked. If they are closed tightly before they are cooked and open after they are cooked, they are good to eat. If a clam does not open when it is cooked, throw it away.

Step 1: Clean clam shells with a bristle brush to remove all dirt and sand. Wash with cold water. (Put on rubber glove or hold towel to protect your hands.)

Step 2: Place clam in palm of hand with hinge near thumb and opening near fingertips. (The thickest part of clam should rest on thickest part of hand.)

Step 3: Open clam with table knife over large bowl to catch juice. Wedge knife between top and bottom shells and slide knife back to cut the muscle at the hinge.

Step 4: Open shell and scrape clam from top into bottom shell. To use juice (liquor), strain through cheesecloth.

See Clam Recipes starting on page 144.

The suggested serving of whole cooked crab is 2 pounds per person which equals about 1 pound after it's cleaned and cracked.

How to Cook Mussels and Clams

Step 1:   Rinse mussels under slowly running water and scrape any critters or mud off the shell. Carefully remove the beard around the edges of the shell.

Step 2:   Discard any mussels that feel heavier than the others. They're probably filled with mud. Discard any mussels with a broken or open shell.

Step 3:   Steam mussels in a large pot with water to cover until shells open, about 8 to 10 minutes. Discard any with unopened shells.

Step 4:   Serve with a butter sauce of white wine and garlic..

How to Prepare Oysters

Step 1:   Discard any oysters with a broken or open shell.

Step 2:   If serving fresh on the half shell, shuck as described for clams on page 137 and serve with cocktail sauce.

Step 3:   Shucked oysters can be baked, sauteed, chopped in chowders and stews, or fried in a light batter.

Geoducks are the largest burrowing clams in the world and can weigh between six and eight pounds. People outside the Pacific Northwest knew little about geoducks until Mike Rowe harvested them on his show "Dirty Jobs". (Geoduck is pronounced "goey duck".)

Friday Harbor Stuffed Crab

¼ bell pepper, seeded, finely diced
1 small onion, finely diced
2 ribs celery, finely diced
¼ cup (½ stick) butter
8 ounces lump crabmeat
1 tablespoon marinade for chicken
1 tablespoon ketchup
1 (8 ounce) carton whipping cream
1 cup seasoned breadcrumbs
Crab shells

- Preheat oven to 350°.

- Saute bell pepper, onion and celery in butter in saucepan and set aside.

- Combine remaining ingredients (except shells) in bowl and add onion-celery mixture.

- Spoon into crab shells and bake for 30 to 35 minutes. Serves 2 to 4.

Cooking twice as much salmon as you need for one meal is always a good idea. There are so many ways to eat the leftovers. Refrigerate remaining salmon, cut it into chunks and serve with a chilled, large pasta tossed with a light salad dressing. Combine salmon chunks with hot pasta, a little dill or garlic and a little extra virgin olive oil or light pesto for a very nice hot entree.

Orcas Island Crab-Angel Pasta

½ cup (1 stick) butter
½ onion, finely chopped
1 bell pepper, seeded, chopped
1 teaspoon dried summer savory
1 teaspoon dried parsley flakes
1 teaspoon dried basil
½ teaspoon celery salt
1 teaspoon lemon pepper
2 (15 ounce) cans diced tomatoes
1 (15 ounce) can Italian stewed tomatoes
½ cup dry white wine
1 pound cooked crabmeat
1 pound angel hair pasta, cooked
Freshly grated parmesan cheese

- Melt butter in large saucepan and saute onion and bell pepper. Stir in summer savory, parsley, basil, celery salt, lemon pepper, ½ teaspoon salt and tomatoes and bring to a boil.

- Add wine and simmer for 5 minutes. Add crabmeat and simmer for 2 minutes.

- Place warm pasta in serving dish and top with crab mixture. Serve with parmesan cheese. Serves 6 to 8.

Washington's San Juan Islands are home to three resident pods of killer whales. More than 85 whales can be seen from May through September from charter boats out of Friday Harbor.

Aberdeen Top-Shelf Tequila Shrimp

1½ pounds medium shrimp, shelled, veined
¼ cup (½ stick) butter
2 tablespoons canola oil
2 cloves garlic, minced
3 tablespoons tequila
1½ tablespoons lime juice
½ teaspoon chili powder
¼ cup coarsely chopped fresh cilantro
Rice, cooked
Lime wedges

- Rinse and pat shrimp dry with paper towels. Heat butter and oil in large skillet over medium heat. Add garlic and shrimp and cook for about 2 minutes, stirring occasionally.

- Stir in tequila, lime juice, ½ teaspoon salt and chili powder. Cook for additional 2 minutes or until most liquid evaporates and shrimp are pink and glazed.

- Add cilantro, serve over rice and garnish with lime wedges. Serves 4 to 6.

Thousands of years ago huckleberries grew in open spaces in the forests of the Pacific Northwest where forest fires cleared areas and let the sun through. Today forest fires continue to clear openings for wild berries of all sorts and keep the forests from overtaking the precious berries.

Fisherman's Beer Shrimp

2 (12 ounce) cans beer
3 tablespoons pickling spice
Lemon slices
2 pounds fresh shrimp

- Pour beer in large stew pot and turn on high heat.

- Add pickling spice, lemon slices and ½ teaspoon salt. When mixture steams, add shrimp and stir well. Make sure there is enough liquid to cover or almost cover shrimp. Add more beer, if necessary.

- Cook just until shrimp turn pink, remove from pot and drain. Serves 4 to 6.

TIP: *For larger amounts, use 1½ to 2 tablespoons pickling spice per pound and enough beer to cover shrimp.*

Commercial fishing accounts for a growing part of the Pacific Northwest's economy and includes salmon, halibut, bottomfish, rockfish, cod, sablefish and smelt. Oysters, crabs and geoduck clams are abundant in the area.

When non-Asian pear production is compared from around the world, Washington ranks eighth and Oregon ranks ninth worldwide.

Olympia Pasta and Shrimp

2 tablespoons butter
1 tablespoon canola oil
½ pound fresh peeled, veined shrimp
½ poblano pepper, seeded, slivered
½ red bell pepper, seeded, sliced
¼ red onion, thinly sliced
1 clove garlic, minced
2 tablespoons snipped cilantro leaves
2 tablespoons tequila or gin
½ teaspoon seasoned salt
¼ teaspoon chili powder
½ teaspoon cumin
⅓ cup half-and-half cream
2 cups cooked angel-hair pasta
Grated parmesan cheese

- Heat butter and oil in large skillet. Add shrimp and cook for about 8 minutes. When shrimp are pink and firm, drain and set aside.

- Add peppers, onion, garlic and cilantro to skillet and saute until just barely tender. Remove vegetables and set aside.

- Add tequila to skillet and swirl it around pan. Add seasoned salt, chili powder, cumin, and half-and-half cream. Allow sauce to thicken slightly.

- Return shrimp and vegetables to skillet and toss until mixture heats well and coats shrimp with cream. Serve immediately over pasta. Garnish with parmesan cheese. Serves 6.

The Grand Coulee Dam on the Columbia River in Washington is the largest dam and concrete structure in the U.S.

Steamed Pacific Littleneck Clams

Pacific littlenecks are small hard-shell clams less
than 2 inches in diameter. They are called "littlenecks"
on the East Coast and Pacific littlenecks on the West Coast.

2 pounds fresh Pacific littleneck clams
4 tablespoons olive oil, divided
4 - 5 cloves garlic, minced
4 green onions with tops, diced
1 cup dry champagne
¼ cup chopped parsley
2 tablespoons lemon juice
½ cup (1 stick) butter

- Wash clams and scrub shells to remove all sand. Pour a little oil into large soup pot and heat over medium-high heat. Saute garlic and onions in hot oil until onions are translucent.

- Pour remaining oil in pot and heat. Add clams, cook for about 2 minutes and toss frequently. Add champagne and cook for additional 3 minutes. Reduce heat, cover and steam for about 5 minutes.

- Remove any clams with open shells and set aside. Continue to cook remaining clams, covered, for additional 5 minutes. Remove all clams with open shells and set aside; discard unopened clams.

- Boil stock in pot until it reduces to about 1 cup. (This may take 5 to 10 minutes.) Simmer and add parsley and lemon juice.

- Drop butter into liquid a little at a time. Continue stirring until butter melts. Taste and season with a little salt and pepper. Pour over clams or serve in bowls for dipping. Serve in shells. Serves 6.

Pacific Northwest Steamers

*These are called Pacific Littlenecks in the Pacific Northwest
and Littlenecks and Cherrystones in the Northeast.*

4 pounds live hard-shelled clams
1¼ cups (2½ sticks) unsalted butter, divided
1 small onion, chopped
4 - 5 cloves garlic, minced
¼ cup snipped parsley
1 teaspoon red pepper flakes
1 bottle white wine
Italian bread

- Scrub shells of clams well to remove sand and grit. Rinse and soak in water and a little kosher or sea salt to remove last bits of grit. (Do not use iodized salt.)

- Add ¼ cup butter to large steamer pot, melt over medium heat and bring to slow boil. Cook onions until translucent. Add garlic, parsley and red pepper flakes and pour wine over all.

- Immediately pour clams into steaming pot, close lid and steam for about 5 to 8 minutes until clams open.

- Remove clams with large slotted spoon or tongs and divide among 4 individual bowls. Discard any clams that do not open. Melt remaining butter and pour into 4 small bowls. Serve clams with melted butter and Italian bread. Serves about 10.

Steelhead trout belong to the family of fish that includes salmon, trout and chars. Steelhead are born in fresh water rivers and migrate to the ocean in their adult stages. Unlike Pacific salmon, steelhead are able to spawn more than once.

Everyday Fried Clams

1 pint fresh, shelled clams
Canola oil
1 cup club soda or beer
¾ cup flour

- Cut large clams into 1 to 1½-inch pieces. Heat oil in deep-fryer or heavy pot to 375°.

- Mix club soda or beer with flour in bowl to make batter. (Add more liquid if needed to get smooth consistency that will stick to clams.)

- Dredge clams through batter and coat well. Carefully drop clams into hot oil and fry for 2 to 3 minutes. Drain on paper towels and keep warm in oven at 250° until ready to serve. Serves 3 to 4.

Easy Grilled Clams

Fresh clams
Butter
Lemon

- Clean all sand and grit from clams and place on grill about 4 to 6 inches from hot coals. Turn clams after 4 minutes and continue to cook until shells open, about 5 minutes longer.

- When shells open, they are ready to eat. Discard clams that do not open. Serve with melted butter and lemon.

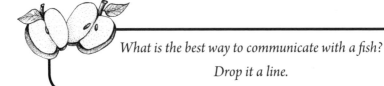

What is the best way to communicate with a fish?

Drop it a line.

Sweets

Cakes • Pies & Cobblers

Cookies & Bars • Desserts

Washington Facts

Mountain Ranges:	*Coast Mountains, Cascades Mountains, Olympic Mountains, Columbia Mountains, Wenatchee Mountains, Blue Mountains, Northern Rocky Mountains*
Five Largest Cities:	*Seattle, Spokane, Tacoma, Vancouver, Bellevue*
National Parks:	*Mount Rainier, Olympic, and North Cascades*

Apple-Date-Walnut Cake

2 cups sugar
1½ cups canola oil
3 eggs
2 teaspoons vanilla
2½ cups flour
1 teaspoon baking soda
1½ teaspoons ground cinnamon
¼ teaspoon ground ginger
3 cups chopped apples
1 (8 ounce) package chopped dates
1 cup chopped walnuts

- Preheat oven to 325°.

- Blend sugar, oil, eggs and vanilla in bowl and beat well. Add flour, baking soda, ½ teaspoon salt, cinnamon and ginger and beat well. Fold in apples, dates and walnuts.

- Pour into 10-inch sprayed, floured tube pan and bake for 1 hour 30 minutes or until toothpick inserted in center comes out clean.

Glaze:

1 cup sugar
1 teaspoon almond extract

- Right before cake is done, bring sugar and 1⅓ cups water in saucepan to a rolling boil and stir constantly. Remove from heat and add almond extract.

- Set aside for 20 minutes; then remove cake from tube pan. Pour glaze over hot cake. Serves 18 to 20.

Best Fresh Apple Cake

1½ cups canola oil
2 cups sugar
3 eggs
2½ cups sifted flour
½ teaspoon baking soda
2 teaspoons baking powder
½ teaspoon ground cinnamon
1 teaspoon vanilla
3 cups peeled, grated apples
1 cup chopped pecans

- Preheat oven to 350°.

- Mix oil, sugar and eggs in bowl and beat well.

- In separate bowl, combine flour, ½ teaspoon salt, baking soda, baking powder and cinnamon. Gradually add flour mixture to creamed mixture.

- Add vanilla, fold in apples and pecans and pour into sprayed, floured tube pan.

- Bake for 1 hour. While cake is still warm, invert onto serving plate.

Glaze:

2 tablespoons butter, melted
2 tablespoons milk
1 cup powdered sugar
1 teaspoon vanilla
¼ teaspoon lemon extract

- Mix all ingredients in bowl and drizzle over cake while cake is still warm. Serves 18 to 20.

Old-Fashioned Applesauce Spice Cake

1 (18 ounce) box spice cake mix
3 eggs
1¼ cups applesauce
⅓ cup canola oil
1 cup chopped pecans
1 (16 ounce) can vanilla frosting
½ teaspoon ground cinnamon

- Preheat oven to 350°.

- Combine cake mix, eggs, applesauce and oil in bowl. Beat on medium speed for 2 minutes. Stir in pecans.

- Pour into sprayed, floured 9 x 13-inch baking pan. Bake for 40 minutes. Cake is done when toothpick inserted in center comes out clean. Cool.

- For a quick frosting, use prepared vanilla frosting and add ½ teaspoon ground cinnamon. Serves 18 to 20.

Blackberries are native to the Northwest and are found from the coast to the mountains on the east and from British Columbia in the north to northern California in the south. They are abundant in burned-out clearings and prairies, but are not grown commercially because of the thorns.

Washington produces more fresh pears than anywhere else in the U.S. Oregon produces the second greatest amount.

Mom's Blackberry Cake

1 (18 ounce) box white cake mix with pudding
1 (3 ounce) package black raspberry gelatin
1 cup canola oil
½ cup milk
4 eggs, beaten
1 cup fresh or frozen blackberries
1 cup flaked coconut
1 cup chopped pecans

- Preheat oven to 350°.

- Combine cake mix, gelatin, oil and milk in bowl and mix well. Add eggs. Fold in blackberries, coconut and pecans. Pour into 3 (9 inch) cake pans.

- Bake for about 45 minutes or until done. Cool before removing from pans.

Frosting:

½ cup (1 stick) butter, softened
1 (1 pound) box powdered sugar
1 cup blackberries
½ cup flaked coconut
½ cup chopped pecans

- Cream butter in bowl and add powdered sugar. Crush blackberries and add to butter-powdered sugar mixture. Add coconut and pecans.

- Frost each layer and stack on top of each other. Use remaining frosting to cover sides. Serves 18 to 20.

Washington's culinary heritage is built on fresh ingredients from local areas and includes seafood, produce and fruits simply prepared without heavy sauces.

Chocolate-Cherry Cake

1 (18 ounce) box milk chocolate cake mix
1 (20 ounce) can cherry pie filling
3 eggs

- Preheat oven to 350°.

- Combine cake mix, pie filling and eggs in bowl and mix with spoon. Pour into sprayed, floured 9 x 13-inch baking dish.

- Bake for 35 to 40 minutes. Cake is done when toothpick inserted in center comes out clean.

Glaze:

5 tablespoons butter
1¼ cups sugar
½ cup milk
1 (6 ounce) package chocolate chips

- When cake is done, combine butter, sugar and milk in medium saucepan. Boil for 1 minute, stirring constantly. Add chocolate chips and stir until chips melt. Pour over hot cake.
  Serves 18 to 20.

"Cherries are a good source of potassium. Increased evidence shows that a diet rich in potassium may help to control blood pressure and reduce the risk for hypertension and stroke." The Washington State Fruit Commission

Nutty Cherry Cake

2 cups sugar
½ cup (1 stick) butter, softened
2 eggs
2½ cups flour
2 teaspoons baking soda
1 (16 ounce) can bing cherries, drained
1 cup chopped pecans

- Preheat oven to 350°.

- Combine sugar, butter and eggs in bowl and beat for several minutes. Add flour and baking soda and mix well. Fold in cherries and pecans.

- Pour into sprayed, floured 9 x 13-inch baking pan and bake for 35 minutes. Cake is done when toothpick inserted in center comes out clean.

Cherry Sauce:

1 (16 ounce) can cherry pie filling
⅓ cup sugar

- Combine cherry pie filling, sugar and ⅓ cup water in saucepan. Heat to dissolve sugar, but not to boiling stage.

- When ready to serve, pour ⅓ cup hot sauce over each piece of cake. Serves 18 to 20.

The cherry season lasts from the first week of June through the end of August. Northwest cherries are harvested, packed and on shelves in two days or less.

Strawberry-Angel Delight Cake

1 cup sweetened condensed milk
¼ cup lemon juice
1 pint fresh strawberries, halved
1 prepared angel food cake
1 (8 ounce) carton whipping cream, whipped

- Combine sweetened condensed milk and lemon juice in bowl. Fold in strawberries.

- Slice cake in half horizontally. Spread strawberry filling on bottom layer and place top layer over filling.

- Cover with whipped cream and top with extra strawberries. Serves 16.

Easy Strawberry Pound Cake

1 (18 ounce) box strawberry cake mix
1 (3.4 ounce) package instant pineapple pudding mix
⅓ cup canola oil
4 eggs
1 (3 ounce) package strawberry gelatin

- Preheat oven to 325°.

- Mix all ingredients plus 1 cup water in bowl and beat for 2 minutes on medium speed.

- Pour into sprayed, floured bundt pan.

- Bake for 55 to 60 minutes. Cake is done when toothpick inserted in center comes out clean.

- Cool for 20 minutes before removing cake from pan. If you would like an icing, use prepared vanilla icing.

TIP: If you like coconut better than pineapple, use coconut cream pudding mix instead of pineapple.

Anchor Cove Kahlua Cake

3 eggs, separated
1¼ cups sugar, divided
½ cup (1 stick) butter, softened
1 cup packed light brown sugar
2¼ cups flour
½ cup cocoa
1½ teaspoons baking soda
⅔ cup strong cold brewed coffee
⅔ cup Kahlua® liqueur

- Preheat oven to 350°.

- Beat egg whites in bowl until frothy, pour in ¾ cup sugar and beat until stiff peaks form. Set aside.

- In separate bowl, cream butter, brown sugar and ½ cup sugar until fluffy. Beat in egg yolks one at a time.

- Sift flour, cocoa and baking soda in bowl. Add to creamed mixture alternately with coffee and Kahlua® liqueur and blend well. Fold egg whites into batter.

- Pour into sprayed, floured bundt pan and bake for 55 to 60 minutes. Cake is done when toothpick inserted in center comes out clean.

- Cool for about 10 to 15 minutes before removing cake from pan. Cool completely before frosting.

Glaze:

1 cup powdered sugar
2 tablespoons cocoa
2 - 3 tablespoons Kahlua® liqueur

- Blend powdered sugar, cocoa and Kahlua® liqueur in bowl, drizzle over top and let some drip down sides of cake. Serves 18 to 20.

Chocolate Regatta Cake

2 cups sugar
2 cups flour
½ cup (1 stick) butter
½ cup canola oil
4 heaping tablespoons cocoa
½ cup buttermilk*
2 eggs, beaten
1 teaspoon baking soda
1 teaspoon ground cinnamon
1 teaspoon vanilla

- Preheat oven to 350°.
- Blend sugar and flour in bowl and set aside.
- Bring butter, oil, cocoa and 1 cup water in saucepan to a boil, pour over flour-sugar mixture and beat well. Add buttermilk, eggs, baking soda, cinnamon, vanilla and ½ teaspoon salt.
- Mix well and pour in sprayed, floured 9 x 13-inch baking pan and bake for 40 to 45 minutes.

Frosting:

½ cup (1 stick) butter, melted
¼ cup cocoa
6 tablespoons milk
1 (1 pound) box powdered sugar
1 teaspoon vanilla
1 cup chopped pecans
1 (7 ounce) can flaked coconut

- Five minutes before cake is done, combine butter, cocoa, milk, powdered sugar and vanilla in bowl and mix well.
- Add pecans and coconut, mix well and spread on hot cake. Serves 18 to 20.

*TIP: To make buttermilk, mix 1 cup milk with 1 tablespoon lemon juice or vinegar and let milk stand for about 10 minutes.

Poppy Seed Cake

3 cups sugar
1¼ cups shortening
6 eggs
3 cups flour
¼ teaspoon baking soda
1 cup buttermilk*
3 tablespoons poppy seeds
2 teaspoons almond extract
2 teaspoons vanilla
2 teaspoons butter flavoring

- Preheat oven to 325°.

- Cream sugar and shortening in large bowl until mixture is light and fluffy. Beat each egg individually, add one at a time to sugar-shortening mixture and blend well after each addition.

- In separate bowl, sift flour, baking soda and ½ teaspoon salt. Alternately add dry ingredients and buttermilk to sugar mixture.

- Add poppy seeds and flavorings and blend well. Pour into sprayed, floured bundt pan. Cook for 1 hour 15 minutes or when toothpick inserted in center comes out clean.

Glaze:

1½ cups powdered sugar
⅓ cup lemon juice
½ teaspoon vanilla
½ teaspoon almond extract

- Combine all ingredients in bowl and mix well. Pour over top of cool cake and let some glaze run down sides of cake. Serves 18.

TIP: To make buttermilk, mix 1 cup milk with 1 tablespoon lemon juice or vinegar and let milk stand for about 10 minutes.

Washington Apple Pie

Piecrust:

2 cups flour
⅔ cup shortening

- Combine flour and ½ teaspoon salt in large bowl. Add shortening a little at a time and stir until lumps are small.

- Slowly pour in 3 tablespoons cold water and stir until it mixes well. Divide dough into 2 pieces and place on floured countertop.

- Roll out each half of dough to about ⅛-inch thick. Place 1 inside 9-inch pie pan. Save remaining half for upper crust.

Pie Filling:

2 tablespoons lemon juice
6 cups peeled, cored, sliced Washington gala or Granny Smith apples
1 cup plus 1 tablespoon sugar
2 tablespoons flour
1½ teaspoons ground cinnamon

- Preheat oven to 375°.

- Sprinkle lemon juice over apples and stir to mix with all slices in bowl. In separate bowl, mix sugar, flour and cinnamon. Pour over apples and stir in.

- Pour pie filling into piecrust. Place second piecrust over top and seal edges of 2 piecrusts. Cut slits in top piecrust. Bake for 60 minutes and cool before serving. Serves 8.

The Washington Apple Commission has a great tip for shoppers. Always choose apples that have shiny skins. Skins that are dull will not be crisp and tasty.

Saucy Spiced Apple Pie

1 (15 ounce) package refrigerated double piecrust
¼ cup (½ stick) butter, softened
2 cups plus 3 tablespoons sugar, divided
1 egg, separated
⅓ cup unsweetened pineapple juice
1½ teaspoons vanilla
⅓ cup flour
½ teaspoon ground cinnamon
¼ teaspoon ground ginger
¼ teaspoon ground nutmeg
6 cups peeled tart apples, sliced

- Preheat oven to 350°.

- Line 9-inch pie pan with 1 piecrust; trim even with edge.

- Cream butter and 2 cups sugar in bowl. Add egg yolk, pineapple juice and vanilla; mix well (mixture will appear curdled).

- In separate bowl, combine flour, cinnamon, ginger and nutmeg; add to creamed mixture. Fill crust with apple slices. Top with creamed mixture.

- Place remaining piecrust over filling. Trim, seal and flute edges. Cut slits in top.

- Beat egg white in bowl; brush over pastry. Sprinkle with remaining sugar.

- Bake for 55 to 60 minutes or until crust is golden brown and filling is bubbly. Cool on wire rack. Refrigerate leftovers. Serves 8.

Americans eat about 19 pounds of fresh apples per person every year. Europeans eat an average of 46 pounds annually.

Fresh Pear Pie a la Mode

1 lemon, halved
5 cups peeled, sliced fresh pears
½ cup sugar
⅓ cup flour
2 tablespoons butter
1 (9-inch) double piecrust
2 tablespoons butter
1 quart vanilla or caramel nonfat frozen yogurt

- Preheat oven to 375°.
- Sprinkle juice of 1 half lemon over pears.
- Mix sugar and flour and carefully fold into pears. Pour mixture into piecrust and top with pats of butter.
- Place top crust over pears, seal edges and cut slits in top. Bake for 40 to 45 minutes. Serve hot with frozen yogurt over top. Serves 8.

Fresh Raspberry Pie

¾ cup sugar
⅓ cup flour
½ cinnamon
⅛ teaspoon allspice, optional
5 cups fresh raspberries
1 (9-inch) double piecrust

- Preheat oven to 400°.
- Mix sugar, flour, cinnamon and allspice in large bowl. Carefully mix in raspberries.
- Place piecrust in 9-inch pie pan and pour berry mixture into crust. Place top crust over berries and seal edges. Cut small slits in top of crust.
- Bake for 45 to 50 minutes. Serves 8.

Creamy Blackberry Pie

4 cups fresh blackberries
1 (9 inch) refrigerated piecrust
1 cup sugar
⅓ cup flour
2 eggs, beaten
½ cup sour cream

- Preheat oven to 350°.

- Place blackberries in piecrust. Combine sugar and flour in bowl.

- In separate bowl, blend eggs and sour cream and add sugar mixture to eggs. Spoon over blackberries.

Topping:

½ cup sugar
½ cup flour
¼ cup (½ stick) butter

- Combine sugar, flour and butter in bowl. Mix well. Crumble evenly over sour cream mixture. Bake for 1 hour or until light brown. Serves 8.

The Sawtooth Berry Fields in Washington's Gifford Pinchot National Forest were reserved as berry fields for the Yakima Indians in 1932. Forest Supervisor K.P. Cecil and Yakima Indian Chief William Yallup shook hands to seal the deal.

Washington produces more raspberries than any other state and accounts for about 90% of the nation's crop.

Easy Creamy Lemon Pie

1 (8 ounce) package cream cheese, softened
1 (14 ounce) can sweetened condensed milk
¼ cup lemon juice
1 (20 ounce) can lemon pie filling
1 (6 ounce) ready graham cracker piecrust

- Beat cream cheese in bowl until smooth and creamy. Add sweetened condensed milk and lemon juice and beat until mixture is creamy.

- Fold in lemon pie filling and stir well. Pour into piecrust and refrigerate for several hours before slicing and serving. Serves 6 to 8.

Washington produces 90% of all red raspberries in the U.S.; 80% of all seed peas; 75% of all hops; 58% of all apples; 47% of all sweet cherries and 42% of all pears grown in the U.S.

Washington is ranked second in the U.S. in the production of lentils, fall potatoes, dry edible peas, asparagus, apricots and sweet corn. And it is ranked third in the production of tart cherries, prunes, plums, summer onions, barley, trout, wheat, cranberries and strawberries.

Pistachio-Lime Pie

2 cups vanilla wafer crumbs
¾ cup chopped pistachio nuts or pecans, divided
¼ cup (½ stick) butter, softened
1 (8 ounce) package cream cheese, softened
1 (14 ounce) can sweetened condensed milk
¼ cup lime juice
1 (3 ounce) package instant pistachio pudding mix
1 (8 ounce) can crushed pineapple with juice
1 (8 ounce) carton whipped topping, thawed

- Preheat oven to 350°.

- Combine crumbs, ¼ cup nuts and butter in bowl and press firmly into 9-inch springform pan. Bake for 8 to 10 minutes and cool.

- Beat cream cheese in large bowl until fluffy, gradually beat in sweetened condensed milk, lime juice and pudding mix and beat until smooth.

- Stir in ½ cup nuts and pineapple and fold in whipped topping.

- Pour into springform pan and refrigerate overnight. Serves 8.

Native Indians who lived in the Pacific Northwest used all the native plants, fruits and wildlife. They spent most of the summer and fall harvesting vegetables, berries and nuts as well as hunting wild game and fishing the abundant rivers. Berries grew in treeless fields and once every few years, they burned the fields to remove trees and weeds so the berries could come back the next year.

Festival Strawberry Cream Cheese Pie

1 (10 ounce) package frozen sweetened strawberries, thawed
2 (8 ounce) packages cream cheese, softened
⅔ cup powdered sugar
1 (8 ounce) carton whipped topping, thawed
1 (6 ounce) ready chocolate piecrust
Fresh strawberries

- Drain strawberries and set aside ¼ cup juice and several strawberries. Combine cream cheese, juice and powdered sugar in bowl and beat well.

- Fold in strawberries and whipped topping and spoon into crust. Refrigerate overnight. Garnish with fresh strawberries to serve. Serves 6 to 8.

White Chocolate Pie

4 (1 ounce) squares white chocolate
20 large marshmallows
½ cup milk
1 (8 ounce) carton whipped topping, thawed
⅔ cup chopped pecans
½ cup maraschino cherries, chopped, well drained
1 (6 ounce) ready graham cracker piecrust

- Melt white chocolate, marshmallows and milk in double boiler. Cool and fold in whipped topping, pecans and cherries.

- Pour into piecrust and freeze. Remove from freezer for 15 minutes before serving. Serves 6 to 8.

Bosc pears are great for cooking because they keep their shape. They have a nutty, buttery flavor and stay yellow after they have ripened.

White Chocolate Cheesecake

2 cups graham cracker crumbs
1 cup slivered almonds, finely chopped
¼ cup (½ stick) butter, softened
8 (1 ounce) squares white chocolate
4 (8 ounce) packages cream cheese, softened
¾ cup sugar
5 eggs
2 tablespoons flour
1 teaspoon vanilla
Strawberries or raspberries
Sugar

- Preheat oven to 275°.

- Combine graham cracker crumbs, almonds and butter in bowl and mix well. Press into 10-inch springform pan. Melt white chocolate in double boiler, stir until smooth and remove from heat.

- Beat cream cheese in bowl until smooth and fluffy and add sugar. Beat in eggs, one at a time, and add flour and vanilla. Mix until smooth and fold in melted white chocolate.

- Pour mixture over graham cracker crust and bake for 60 minutes or until top is firm.

- Cool completely, cover and refrigerate overnight. Slice strawberries (leave raspberries whole), sprinkle on a little sugar and refrigerate overnight.

- To serve, remove sides of springform pan. Spoon ¼ cup fruit over each slice of cheesecake. You should get about 16 slices of cheesecake. Serves 10 to 12.

TIP: *The best way to slice cheesecake is to use a sharp knife, clean after each slice, then dip in water before slicing the next piece.*

Wind-in-the-Sails Cheesecake

1¼ cups graham cracker crumbs
½ cup flaked coconut
½ cup chopped pecans
2 tablespoons light brown sugar
¼ cup (½ stick) butter, melted
2 (8 ounce) packages cream cheese, softened
1 (14 ounce) can sweetened condensed milk
3 eggs
¼ cup frozen orange juice concentrate, thawed
1 teaspoon pineapple extract
1 (20 ounce) can pineapple pie filling, divided
1 cup sour cream

- Preheat oven to 300°.

- Mix graham cracker crumbs, coconut, pecans, brown sugar and butter in bowl. Press firmly into 9-inch springform pan and set aside.

- Beat cream cheese in large bowl until fluffy. Gradually beat in sweetened condensed milk.

- Add eggs one at a time, juice concentrate and pineapple extract and mix well. Stir in ¾ cup pineapple pie filling.

- Pour into sprayed springform pan. Bake for 1 hour or until center sets.

- Spread top with sour cream and bake for additional 5 minutes. Cool, spread remaining pineapple pie filling over cheesecake and refrigerate. Serves 10 to 12.

Raw Anjou and Comice pears are excellent served with cheeses. They are some of the sweetest, juiciest varieties.

Washington Apple Crisp

5 cups peeled, cored, sliced apples
½ cup (1 stick) butter, melted
1 cup quick-cooking oats
½ cup firmly packed brown sugar
⅓ cup flour

- Preheat over to 375°.

- Place apple slices in 8-inch or 9-inch square baking pan.

- Combine butter, oats, brown sugar and flour in bowl and sprinkle mixture over apples.

- Bake for 40 to 45 minutes or until apples are tender and topping is golden brown. Serves 9.

TIP: For a change, add 1 teaspoon cinnamon and ½ cup raisins or dried cranberries to apples before sprinkling with topping.

Cinnamon-Apple Cobbler

2 (20 ounce) cans apple pie filling
½ cup packed brown sugar
1½ teaspoons ground cinnamon
1 (18 ounce) box yellow cake mix
½ cup (1 stick) butter, melted

- Preheat oven to 350°.

- Spread apple pie filling in sprayed 10 x 15-inch baking dish.

- Sprinkle with brown sugar and cinnamon and top with dry cake mix. Drizzle melted butter over top of cake mix.

- Bake for 50 minutes or until light brown and bubbly. Serves 16.

Black Bear Blueberry Buckle

Excellent for brunch!

2 cups flour
3 cups sugar
2 teaspoons baking powder
1 egg
½ cup milk
¼ cup (½ stick) butter, softened
2 cups blueberries

- Preheat oven to 375°.

- Combine flour, sugar, baking powder, egg, ½ teaspoon salt, milk and butter in large bowl. Fold in blueberries carefully.

- Spread in sprayed 9-inch square baking pan and set aside.

Topping:

¼ cup (½ stick) butter, softened
⅓ cup flour
½ cup sugar
½ teaspoon ground cinnamon

- Combine butter, flour, sugar and cinnamon in bowl and sprinkle over blueberry mixture

- Bake for 30 to 35 minutes. Serve warm. Serves 8 to 10.

Washington state claims 90% of the U.S. production of raspberries. Raspberries can be deep purple, red, black or golden yellow. Hybrids of raspberries include boysenberries and loganberries.

Easy Cherry Cobbler

2 (20 ounce) cans cherry pie filling
1 (18 ounce) box white cake mix
¾ cup (1½ sticks) butter, melted
2 (2 ounce) packages slivered almonds
Whipped topping, thawed

- Preheat oven to 350°.

- Spread pie filling in sprayed 9 x 13-inch baking pan. Sprinkle cake mix over pie filling.

- Drizzle butter over top and sprinkle with almonds. Bake for 45 minutes. Top with whipped topping to serve. Serves 16.

Double-Berry Cobbler

1 (12 ounce) package frozen raspberries
1 (12 ounce) package frozen blackberries
⅓ cup sugar
⅓ cup flour
¼ cup (½ stick) butter, melted
½ (15 ounce) package refrigerated piecrust

- Preheat oven to 375°.

- Combine raspberries, blackberries, sugar, flour and butter in large bowl and mix well.

- Spoon berry mixture into sprayed 9 x 13-inch baking dish.

- Roll 1 piecrust to fit on top of berry mixture and sprinkle with extra sugar.

- Bake for 1 hour or until golden brown and bubbly. Serves 16.

Apple Tarts

1 (10 ounce) package frozen puff pastry shells
½ cup Craisins®
¼ cup apple brandy
¼ cup sugar
1 (20 ounce) can apple pie filling
½ teaspoon cinnamon

- Preheat oven to 400°.

- Place pastry shells on baking sheet and bake for 20 minutes. Cool shells before adding filling.

- Combine Craisins®, apple brandy and sugar in saucepan and let soak for 10 minutes.

- Add pie filling and cinnamon to saucepan and mix well. Fill each pastry shell with pie mixture. Serve immediately or chilled. Serves 8.

TIP: If you like, serve the tarts with a dollop of whipped topping or a scoop of vanilla ice cream.

Juan Perez sailed north from San Blas, Mexico along the Pacific Coast in 1774 and claimed all the land south of Russian America (Alaska) for Spain. He made the first European record of the Northwest coast.

British explorer James Cook named Cape Flattery in Washington in 1778. His reports encouraged European fur trappers and traders to come by sea and land.

Homestead Date-Pecan Tarts

1 (8 ounce) package pitted, chopped dates
1½ cups milk
½ cup flour
1½ cups sugar
3 eggs, beaten
1 teaspoon vanilla
1 cup chopped pecans
8 tart shells, baked, cooled
1 (8 ounce) carton whipping cream
3 tablespoons powdered sugar

- Combine dates, milk, flour and sugar in heavy saucepan and cook for about 3 minutes, stirring constantly.

- Slowly stir in eggs and ¼ teaspoon salt and continue cooking, stirring constantly, for additional 5 minutes. Stir in vanilla and pecans. Pour into baked tart shells and cool.

- Whip cream in bowl, add powdered sugar, top each tart with whipped cream and refrigerate. Serves 8.

The first weather-related event recorded in the Pacific Northwest was by the Japanese writing about a tsunami caused by an earthquake in the Pacific Northwest in 1700. This record confirmed the discovery by geologists and the oral history provided by Native Americans.

Almond-Fudge Shortbread

1 cup (2 sticks) butter, softened
1 cup powdered sugar
1¼ cups flour
1 (12 ounce) package chocolate chips
1 (14 ounce) can sweetened condensed milk
½ teaspoon almond extract
1 (2.5 ounce) package chopped almonds, toasted

- Preheat oven to 350°.

- Beat butter, powdered sugar and ¼ teaspoon salt in bowl and stir in flour. Pat into sprayed 9 x 13-inch baking pan and bake for 15 minutes.

- Melt chocolate chips with sweetened condensed milk in medium saucepan over low heat and stir until chips melt. Stir in almond extract.

- Spread evenly over shortbread and sprinkle with almonds. Refrigerate for several hours or until firm and cut into bars. They may be stored at room temperature. Yields 2 dozen cookies.

Chinese Cookies

1 (6 ounce) package chocolate chips
1 (6 ounce) package butterscotch chips
1 cup salted peanuts
1 (3 ounce) can chow mein noodles

- Melt chocolate and butterscotch chips in large saucepan over low heat. Add peanuts and noodles and mix well.

- Drop by teaspoonfuls onto wax paper. Refrigerate just to harden. Yields 2 dozen cookies.

Mountain Nuggets

1 cup (2 sticks) butter, softened
1 cup packed brown sugar
1½ cups sugar
1 tablespoon milk
2 teaspoons vanilla
2 eggs
1 cup crushed corn flakes
3 cups quick-cooking oats
1½ cups flour
1 teaspoon baking soda
2 teaspoons ground cinnamon
¼ teaspoon ground nutmeg
⅛ teaspoon ground cloves
½ cup flaked coconut
2 cups chocolate chips
1 cup chopped pecans

- Preheat oven to 350°.

- Cream butter, brown sugar and sugar in large bowl and beat in milk, vanilla and eggs. Stir in corn flakes and oats.

- In separate bowl, sift flour, baking soda, 1 teaspoon salt and spices. Gradually add to cookie mixture. (Cookie batter will be very stiff.)

- Stir in coconut, chocolate chips and pecans. Drop teaspoonfuls of dough onto cookie sheet. Bake for 10 to 15 minutes. Yields 5 dozen cookies.

The Washington Territory was formed from the Oregon Territory in 1853. Oregon became a state in 1859 and Washington became a state in 1889.

Crunchy Cashew Cookies

1 cup (2 sticks) butter, softened
1 cup sugar
¾ cup packed brown sugar
1 egg
2¼ cups flour
½ teaspoon baking soda
½ teaspoon cream of tartar
2 teaspoons vanilla
1 teaspoon almond extract
1½ cups chopped cashews

- Preheat oven to 350°.

- Combine butter, sugar, brown sugar and egg in bowl and beat well. Blend in flour, baking soda and cream of tartar. Add vanilla, almond extract and cashews and mix thoroughly.

- Drop teaspoonfuls of dough onto sprayed cookie sheet and bake for 10 to 12 minutes or until golden brown. Yields 3 dozen cookies.

Thousands of years ago huckleberries grew in open spaces in the forests of the Pacific Northwest where forest fires cleared areas and let the sun through. Today forest fires continue to clear openings for wild berries of all sorts and keep the forests from overtaking the precious berries.

The first soft-serve ice cream machine was used in a Dairy Queen in Olympia, Washington.

Macadamia Nut Cookies

½ cup shortening
½ cup (1 stick) butter, softened
2½ cups flour, divided
1 cup packed brown sugar
½ cup sugar
2 eggs
1 teaspoon vanilla
½ teaspoon butter flavoring
½ teaspoon baking soda
1 (12 ounce) package white chocolate chips
1 (3 ounce) jar macadamia nuts, chopped

- Preheat oven to 350°.
- Beat shortening and butter in bowl. Add half flour and mix well. Add brown sugar, sugar, eggs, vanilla, butter flavoring and baking soda.
- Beat until mixture combines well. Add remaining flour, mix well and stir in white chocolate chips and nuts.
- Drop teaspoonfuls of dough onto cookie sheet and bake for 8 minutes. Yields 3 dozen cookies.

Orange Balls

1 (12 ounce) box vanilla wafers, crushed
½ cup (1 stick) butter, melted
1 (16 ounce) box powdered sugar
1 (6 ounce) can frozen orange juice concentrate, thawed
1 cup finely chopped pecans

- Combine vanilla wafers, butter, powdered sugar and orange juice concentrate in bowl and mix well.
- Roll into balls and roll in chopped pecans. Store in airtight container. Yields 1½ dozen balls.

Apricot-Almond Bars

1 (18 ounce) box yellow cake mix
½ cup (1 stick) butter, melted
¾ cup finely chopped almonds
1 (12 ounce) jar apricot preserves, slightly heated, divided
1 (8 ounce) package cream cheese, softened
¼ cup sugar
2 tablespoons flour
1 egg
1 teaspoon vanilla
⅔ cup flaked coconut

- Combine cake mix and butter in large bowl and mix with spoon until crumbly. Stir in almonds and set aside 1 cup crumb mixture.

- Lightly press crumb mixture into sprayed 9 x 13-inch baking pan. Carefully spread 1 cup preserves over crumb mixture, leaving ¼-inch border.

- Beat cream cheese in bowl until smooth and add remaining preserves, sugar, flour, ⅛ teaspoon salt, egg and vanilla. Carefully spread cream cheese mixture over preserves.

- In separate bowl, combine remaining 1 cup crumb mixture and coconut and mix well. Sprinkle over cream cheese mixture and bake for 35 minutes or until center sets. Cool and store in refrigerator. Yields 20 bars.

A cut piece of apple or orange in a cookie jar keeps cookies moist.

Macadamia Bars

Crust:

1 cup (2 sticks) butter, softened
⅔ cup sugar
2 cups flour

- Preheat oven to 350°.

- Cream butter, sugar and flour in bowl. Press into sprayed 9 x 13-inch baking dish and bake for 20 minutes.

Filling:

4 eggs
1 cup flaked coconut
3 cups packed light brown sugar
2 (3.2 ounce) jars macadamia nuts, chopped
¼ cup flour
3 teaspoons vanilla extract
1 teaspoon baking powder

- Lightly beat eggs in medium bowl and add remaining filling ingredients. Pour over hot, baked crust and bake for additional 25 to 30 minutes.

- Cool completely and cut into small squares or you can cut in larger squares and serve with dip of ice cream. Yields 20 bars.

TIP: *You could substitute 1½ cups walnuts for macadamia nuts. Either way, these bars are moist, chewy and absolutely sinful.*

The Washington border on the north is adjacent to British Columbia, Canada and runs along the 49th parallel except for Vancouver Island. It borders Oregon to the south. This border runs along the 46th parallel and the Columbia River.

Almond-Coconut Squares

2 cups graham cracker crumbs
3 tablespoons brown sugar
½ cup (1 stick) butter, melted
1 (14 ounce) can sweetened condensed milk
1 (7 ounce) package shredded coconut
1 teaspoon vanilla

- Preheat oven to 325°.

- Combine graham cracker crumbs, brown sugar and butter in bowl and mix well. Pat mixture evenly into sprayed 9 x 13-inch baking pan and bake for 10 minutes. Cool.

- Combine sweetened condensed milk, coconut and vanilla in bowl and pour over baked crust. Bake for additional 25 minutes. Cool.

Topping:

1 (6 ounce) package chocolate chips
1 (6 ounce) package butterscotch chips
¼ cup (½ stick) butter
6 tablespoons crunchy peanut butter
½ cup slivered almonds

- Melt all topping ingredients in double boiler and spread mixture over baked ingredients. Cool and cut into squares. Yields 20 squares.

Olympia is the capital of Washington and is considered one of the most beautiful state capital settings in the U.S. Olympia sits on Budd Inlet which connects to Puget Sound and has picturesque views of Mount Rainier and the Olympic Mountain Range.

Buttery Walnut Squares

1 cup (2 sticks) butter, softened
1¾ cups packed brown sugar
1¾ cups flour

- Preheat oven to 350°.

- Combine butter and brown sugar in bowl and beat until smooth and creamy. Add flour and mix well. Pat mixture down evenly in sprayed 9 x 13-inch glass pan and bake for 15 minutes.

Topping:

1 cup packed brown sugar
4 eggs, lightly beaten
2 tablespoons flour
2 cups chopped walnuts
1 cup flaked coconut

- Combine sugar and eggs in medium bowl. Add flour and mix well. Fold in walnuts and coconut and pour over crust.

- Bake for 20 to 25 minutes or until set in center. Cool in pan and cut into squares. Yields 20 squares.

TIP: Serve these delicious squares with a scoop of ice cream for a great dessert.

Mount Rainier in Washington is the tallest mountain in the Cascade Range and can be seen on a clear day from as far as 100 miles away.

Valley Apple Dumplings

1½ cups firmly packed brown sugar, divided
¼ cup chopped pecans
2 tablespoons butter, softened
6 baking apples, cored
1 (15 ounce) package refrigerated double piecrust

- Preheat oven to 425°.

- Mix ½ cup packed brown sugar, pecans and butter in bowl and spoon mixture into each apple.

- Roll both piecrusts to ⅛-inch thickness. Cut into 6 squares approximately 7 inches each.

- Wrap 1 square around each apple, pinch edges to seal and place in baking dish.

- Place remaining 1 cup packed brown sugar and ½ cup water in saucepan over medium heat and stir until sugar dissolves. Pour syrup over dumplings.

- Bake for 35 to 40 minutes or until tender and baste occasionally with syrup. Serves 6.

TIP: *For even more flavorful dumplings, add 2 teaspoons ground cinnamon or apple pie spice along with sugar, pecans and butter.*

Washington's economy is dominated by aviation, software and technology, wheat, apples, beans and other agriculture, forest products, and fishing. Washington is a major exporter of manufactured goods, foodstuffs, raw materials and hydroelectricity.

Caramel-Apple Mousse

¾ cup (1½ sticks) butter
⅔ cup plus ¼ cup sugar, divided
2½ teaspoons lemon juice
½ teaspoon ground cinnamon
2 tablespoons rum
5 - 6 medium apples, peeled, thinly sliced
1 teaspoon vanilla
1 (8 ounce) carton whipped topping, thawed
Peanut brittle, slightly crushed

- Melt butter in large skillet and add ⅔ cup sugar, lemon juice and ¼ cup water. Cook for 10 minutes or until sugar dissolves and syrup is slightly thick and golden; stir often. Remove from heat and add cinnamon, rum and apples.

- Return to heat and cook apples in syrup for 5 to 6 minutes or until they are thoroughly coated and soft. Remove apples from syrup and cool.

- In separate bowl, add ¼ cup sugar and vanilla to whipped topping and fold apples into whipped topping. Spoon mixture into parfait or crystal sherbet glasses and refrigerate for several hours.

- Sprinkle generously with crushed peanut brittle before serving. Serves 8.

The state of Washington is the only state to be named after an American president.

Mango Cream

2 ripe, soft mangoes
½ gallon vanilla ice cream, softened
1 (6 ounce) can frozen lemonade concentrate, thawed
1 (8 ounce) carton whipped topping, thawed

- Peel mangoes, cut slices around seed and chop slices. Mix ice cream, lemonade concentrate and whipped topping in large bowl and fold in mango chunks.

- Quickly spoon mixture into parfait glasses, cover with plastic wrap and freeze. Serves 8 to 10.

Toffee-Cream Surprise

1 cup buttermilk*
1 (3 ounce) package French vanilla instant pudding
1 (12 ounce) carton whipped topping, thawed
1 (12 ounce) package toffee toppers, fudge covered, shortbread cookies
1 (10 ounce) jar maraschino cherries, drained, halved
1 cup chopped pecans
1 cup miniature marshmallows

- Combine buttermilk and vanilla pudding in bowl. Beat with whisk until it mixes thoroughly. Fold in whipped topping.

- Lightly crumble cookies with knife blade of food processor. Don't pulverize cookies. You may have to break a few cookies up by hand. Leave some cookies in chunks.

- Fold cookies, cherries, pecans and marshmallows into pudding mixture. Refrigerate in covered bowl and serve in individual sherbet dishes. Best served same day. Serves 12.

*TIP: To make buttermilk, mix 1 cup with 1 tablespoon lemon juice or vinegar and let milk stand for about 10 minutes.

Ice Cream with Hot Raspberry Sauce

2 pints fresh raspberries
¾ cup sugar
2 tablespoons cornstarch
Ice cream

- Soak raspberries with sugar in ½ cup water in saucepan for about 20 minutes. Pour small amount of water from raspberries into small cup. Add cornstarch and stir well to dissolve cornstarch.

- Pour raspberries and cornstarch mixture into blender and process to desired consistency. Strain over saucepan while pouring processed raspberries into saucepan.

- Bring to a boil, reduce heat to low and cook for 2 to 4 minutes or until sauce thickens; stir constantly. Serve over ice cream. Serves 4.

Coffee Surprise

1 (10 ounce) package large marshmallows
1 cup strong brewed coffee
1 (8 ounce) package chopped dates
1¼ cups chopped pecans
1 (8 ounce) carton whipping cream, whipped

- Melt marshmallows in hot coffee. Add dates and pecans and refrigerate.

- When mixture thickens, fold in whipped cream.

- Pour into 6 sherbet glasses. Place plastic wrap over top and refrigerate. Serves 6.

TIP: *This is a super dessert – no slicing, no "dishing up" – just bring it right from the fridge to the table.*

Bibliography

A Field Guide to Pacific State Wildflowers: Washington, Oregon, California and Adjacent Areas. Theodore F. Niehaus, Charles Ripper, Roger Tory Peterson. Peterson Field Guides 1998.

A Sierra Club Naturalist's Guide to the Pacific Northwest. Stephen Whitney. Sierra Club, 1989

Access Washington: Official State Government Web site   www.access.wa.gov/

Atlas of the Pacific Northwest. Philip L. Jackson. Oregon State University, 1993

Enchanted Learning   www.enchantedlearning.com/usa/states/

Farthest Frontier: The Pacific Northwest. Sidney Warren. Macmillan Co., 1949

50 States   www.50states.com

Fodor's Pacific Northwest. Eric B. Wechter. Fodor's Travel Publications, Inc. 2008

Frommer's Washington State (Frommer's Complete). Karl Swanson. Wiley 2008.

Hidden Pacific Northwest: Including Oregon, Washington, Vancouver, Victoria. Eric Lucas, Richard Harris, Stephen Dolainshki, John Gottberg. Ulyssses Press, 2007

Historical Atlas of the Pacific Northwest: Maps of Exploration and Discovery. Derek Hayes. Sasquatch Books, 1999.

Lonely Planet: Washington, Oregon and the Pacific Northwest. Sandra Bao, Brendan Sainsbury. Lonely Planet Travel Guides 2008

Official Site of Washington State Tourism   www.tourism.wa.gov

Pacific Northwest   www.wikipedia.org/wiki/Pacific_Northwest

Pacific Northwest Travel Guide   www.gonorthwest.com

Pacific Northwest History   www.lib.washington.edu/sugject/History/tm/pmw.html

The Heart of the Red Firs: A Story of the Pacific Northwest. Ada Woodruff Anderson. Little, Brown and Company

The Washington Almanac: Facts About Washington. Andrea Jarvela. Westwinds Press 2003.

Washington State Travel   www.washingtonstate.worldweb.com

Washington, A Guide In The Evergreen State. Washington Writer's Project of the Work Projects Administration and American Guide Series 1941.

Washington Atlas and Gazetteer. Delorme 2006.

Washington Guide to the Evergreen State. American Guide Series; Federal Writers Project 1989

Washington State Fishing Guide (8th Edition); Terry Sheely; TNS Communications Publication; 2001.

Washington's History: The People, Land and Events of the Far Northwest. Harry Ritter. Westwinds Press 2003.

Wikipedia   www.en.wikipedia.org

Index

190   Recipes from Washington